Letters to Missionaries
Volume I

Preparing to Embark in the Service of God

WILLIAM HAYES PINGREE

Praetorius Publishers, LLC

© 2014 Praetorius Publishers, LLC

www.praetoriuspublishers.com

All rights reserved. No part of this book may be reproduced in any form or by any means without permission in writing from the publisher, Praetorius Publishers, LLC; P.O. Box 9113; Salt Lake City, Utah 84109-0113. The views expressed herein are the responsibility of the author and do not necessarily represent the position of Praetorius Publishers, LLC.

Library of Congress Cataloging-in-Publication Data

William Hayes Pingree, author
Letters to Missionaries: Preparing to Embark in the Service of God / Volume I / William Hayes Pingree
      pages cm
      Includes bibliographical references
      ISBN 978-0-9910147-1-2 (paperbound: alk. paper)

Library of Congress Number: 2014958212

Printed in the United States of America

10 9 8 7 6 5 4 3 2 1

This work is dedicated to the 162 missionaries who undertook the missionary preparation course, learned the principles and doctrines of the gospel and successfully implemented these into their missions...

CONTENTS OF VOLUME I

PREFACE.. i

ACKNOWLEDGEMENTS.. v

INTRODUCTION... vii

LETTER ONE
Prologue To Missionary Service – Why You Have Been Called... 1

LETTER TWO
Preparation: The Need To Be Worthy................................... 17

LETTER THREE
The First Lesson Of Successful Missionary Service............... 31

LETTER FOUR
The MTC And The Second Important Lesson To Learn......... 44

LETTER FIVE
The Third Most Valuable Lesson – Avoiding Pride................ 51

LETTER SIX
Missionaries Must Understand The Doctrine Of Grace, Agency And Justified Works... 67

LETTER SEVEN
As Missionaries, What Are We To Do And What Is The Lord To Do.. 90

LETTER EIGHT
What Is The Relationship Between Faith, Knowledge, And Obedience?... 114

LETTER NINE
Why Faith Must Precede Obedience... 130

LETTER TEN
Why Priesthood Keys Are Vital.. 139

LETTER ELEVEN
The Right Must Serve The Good... 174

BIBLIOGRAPHY... 187

"Therefore, O ye that embark in the service of God, see that ye serve him with all your heart, might, mind and strength, that ye may stand blameless before God at the last day."

Doctrine and Covenants 4:2

PREFACE

As the times and seasons have changed, the approach to "preaching the gospel" has been reworked over and over again so that the results of such efforts are more productive. This then should ensure greater success in such an endeavor. It is often hoped that those who bear the message of the restored gospel will adapt themselves to this evolving new methodology and thus ensure the realization of the goal that more of our Father in Heaven's children will embrace the message of salvation and join the church. While such goals are laudatory even as they do indeed produce a better-trained self, the attainment of such often comes at a high cost, the undernourishment of the soul of the messenger. As a professor of international relations and political theory at the University of Utah, I was a teacher first and foremost for almost twenty years, winning the Professor of Choice Award and other accolades. Starting in 1995, I taught a missionary course helping prepare young missionaries to serve all over the world. For ten of those years, I also taught courses in the Book of Mormon, the New Testament and the Pearl of Great Price at the LDS Institute of Religion at the University of Utah.

Teaching is more than a process and as I taught missionary preparation, I sought after the matters of the soul, for although matters of the self are necessary, they are certainly insufficient in preparing missionaries. While matters of the self should not be ignored, it is the elements pertaining to the soul that are truly "the weightier matters" when it comes to missionary preparation, as indicated by our Savior in Matthew 23:23. It was part of these preparation courses that we learned in-depth the doctrines of the restored gospel. By integrating these lessons with meaningful practice, the souls of these young missionaries would be reordered according to the priorities and practices the Savior Himself had established. His mission was to be our mission; His practices of nourishing the soul in priority to matters of the self were to be learned and carried out. The missionary preparation class took one year and in due course, we came to the Christmas season, the perfect time to both learn and teach the ennobling doctrines of salvation. It is a time where doctrine can be practiced and souls can be enlarged, something every missionary must come to understand.

It was at this time that my students undertook an uncommon pursuit, one that would nourish the soul more than the self. We would hold a Christmas dinner for those who were much less fortunate than we were. The potential candidates for such a dinner were everywhere. This meal was held in my home, with the mothers of the potential missionaries preparing the food. It would include turkey, ham, roasted and mashed potatoes and gravy, yams, vegetables, and of course, wassail, and Christmas pudding. Each student was to prayerfully invite someone who found themselves in the conditions above described. The way this event was to be carried out had been given to us by Elder David B. Haight, a member of the Quorum of the Twelve (1906-2004). As he had returned to activity in the church, the matters of the soul weighed heavily on his heart. He too decided to invite those who were indigent to a Christmas feast at his home.

According to Elder Haight's example, we in a like manner prepared invitations to the dinner that read, "Our Savior would like you to come to Christmas dinner." We then gave my address as the location for the dinner and the person who gave the invitation was listed as the sponsor of the invitee to the dinner. As was to be expected, the entitled invitation sparked unusual interest, and none of those so invited ever turned the invitation away. Over the years, we had very inactive attendees, those who were encrusted with great sin and even on two occasions, homeless men were invited who were begging for money at Temple Square. No judgment of their circumstances was ever rendered; all were welcomed and thanked for their attendance.

As they came, many were picked up and brought by my students, they were apprehensive and filled with fear as to what to expect from such a dinner. Many were underfed physically and all were undernourished spiritually. We made them feel comfortable and fed them on the finest china and stemware. As our guests began to relax, curiosity overtook the angst displayed on their arrival, and they began to wonder why such an invitation was extended and what did it have to do with our Savior, Jesus Christ? As we finished our dinner and moved on to dessert, we gathered in the family room and were warmed by an inviting fire. It was then that I asked each member of our group to explain to the others what the Savior specifically had done for them that past year. Each was to explain how the direct intervention of our Lord had blessed their lives. There were many tender moments and as I watched our guests, wonderment crept across their faces. Finally, I indicated that they too might respond to the same question, should they desire to do so. Many declined, but a surprising number began to tell us how specifically the Lord had responded to them, even under conditions that could not be construed other than rebellion or disobedience.

There was not a dry eye in the room and tender feelings were shared; moments of inspiration and revelation began to sink deeply into the souls of all who were present. The Spirit of God descended upon all of us as we realized the clear reality of the Savior's mission. He was there to save all mankind, not just those who now embraced His gospel, but His message was for all and He invited all to partake. He was omnipresent in an intimate and personal manner that was hidden to us unless we sought after His presence. Doctrine and practice came together that night powerfully in ways never to be forgotten and souls were enlarged and healed in ways that had universal application to missionary work for all time. It is because of times like these that I have left the preparation of the self to those better suited to undertake such tasks; those who have mastered these skills of behavior modification have triumphed stunningly and these skills are essential and scientifically self-affirming. However, the art of learning the doctrines of the restoration through the Spirit and how to apply them are matters of the soul and have been left to experiences such as those described above. We have refined the training of the self to a fine science, while the art of reordering the soul and the integration of these doctrines into our very beings must be left to rigorous doctrinal study tempered by the expression of love found in serving in the way of the Master. It is to that end, to the preparation of the soul, that the letters found in this book, *Letters to Missionaries, Volume I – Preparing to Embark in the Service of God*, is dedicated.

ACKNOWLEDGEMENTS

Missionary work in the Church of Jesus Christ of Latter-day Saints is not for the faint of heart and there are many moving parts in trying to prepare a primer for young men and women who seek the abundant life found in missionary service. Today's young missionaries face a daunting task of preparing themselves to be equal to the responsibilities they assume upon entering the service of the church. Great effort is expended in preparing the self, but for the matters of the soul, this has been left somewhat unattended. To respond to this need, tending to matters of the soul, there are many who have shared this vision, and they deserve a great deal of thanks.

I would like to thank the editors and staff of Praetorius Publishers, in particular Alan Monsen, for helping make this book possible. With his invaluable support, rock solid belief and diligence, this book was able to leave the idea realm and become a reality in a standardized user-friendly format to benefit all missionaries. I would further like to thank Ron Case, currently an instructor at the University of Utah's Institute of Religion. Brother Case and I were colleagues when I taught at the Institute for so many years, and he currently teaches missionary preparation there. His edits and efforts to make the book better found in me a willing student as he made suggestions on doctrine and practice that were invaluable.

This book has been dedicated to the young men who were my students in the missionary preparation course. At that time, sisters had not responded in such numbers to serve in the mission field. Today, however, there are a great number of worthy sisters who have entered missionary service with great effect. They, as well as the numerous young men who are now responding to a call to serve will benefit greatly from the letters contained in this book. At the time I taught mission preparation, men were charged then as today with the priesthood responsibility of preaching the gospel.

It was my privilege to teach 162 extraordinary young men who made a great difference to the missions in which they served. These remarkable young men were able to ask searching questions due to a deep and abiding curiosity to learn the doctrines of the restoration. This desire to learn, along with their well-framed inquiries provided the opportunity to correspond with them as they searched for a greater relevant knowledge of the gospel. The relevance for which they sought is discovered in the answers found in this book. To them then, who had the courage to ask, we all owe a great debt of gratitude.

I have followed these young men as they left the missionary service. They acquitted themselves well as they found their missions were enhanced by celestial service, truly they were shaped by the touch of the Master's hand. As they learned to attend to the matters of the soul, even early on in their missionary experience, such attention has become a pattern for them. This learning, which began early in their missionary service, as explored in Volume I, became a template for their future lives. By attending to the matters of the soul, their service in the cause of Christ was not only deepened, but has been multiplied a thousand fold when they returned home.

A teacher pours his or her life into the lives of their students. Efforts to acquire worldly wealth and success are eclipsed by the joy that is found in watching students, those like these great young men, embrace with enthusiasm the things they know to be true. In my case, I am rich beyond the horizons found in worldly pursuits and as I rejoice in the accomplishments of these young men, I am overwhelmed with gratitude for the important times we spent together teaching, learning and counseling together. It is to our Heavenly Father that I am the most grateful for this experience captured in the pages of this book.

INTRODUCTION

Beginning in the late 1960's, missionaries for the Church of Jesus Christ of Latter day Saints, with a mission requiring a foreign language, began to prepare themselves linguistically before they entered their fields of labor. There were certain missions, requiring a language, where missionaries were required to attend the Language Training Mission. At the MTC, the well known "six discussions" were learned in he anguage f heir ission. The three original languages represented then were Spanish, Portuguese, and German. By March of 1971, in the *Church News,* it was reported that:

> Each year more than two thousand newly called missionaries – both elders and sisters – begin the intensive first eight week of their mission experience in the Language Training missions. Missionaries learning Spanish, Portuguese, German, Navaho, French, Italian, and Afrikaans attend the Language Training Mission at Provo, Utah. The Dutch, Danish, Finnish, Swedish, and Norwegian languages are taught at Rexburg, Idaho. In Laie, Hawaii, missionaries study Japanese, Cantonese, Mandarin, Samoan, Tongan, Korean, and Tahitian.

In the forty some years since this article appeared, the two thousand missionaries found in the Language Training Mission has exploded to over 40,000 missionaries every year who now attend Missionary Training Centers throughout the world. The curriculum has also changed during this time. Now, even those who will teach the gospel in English attend these various Missionary Training Centers so that they may be instructed in teaching methodology and practice, skills at overcoming objections to the message, and useful role plays in how to put such things into practice. These skills are very useful and help uninitiated young men and women to have a productive institutional experience when they later encounter an ever increasing secular world. These are learned skills pertinent to matters of the "self."

Originally, at the Language Training Missions, it was recognized that many missionaries were doctrinally unprepared to confront a more or less knowledgeable and believing public in their respective fields of labor. Thus, to enhance their gospel knowledge, and to take advantage of the three month training, time was split between learning the "six discussions" and scriptural discussion courses. The former prepared the "self" to teach, the latter prepared the "soul" to learn and to be nourished by the good word of God. In these courses, the doctrines of the restoration were taught and explained by those returned missionaries who had been called to inspire their eager fellow servants. These courses followed a week of General Authority instruction at the Salt Lake Mission Home, located in downtown Salt Lake City, where all missionaries received counsel and instruction from modern apostles and other general officers of the church. The topics ranged from what was expected of the missionaries to what they should teach. It was a most inspiring time where testimony was born by these servants of the Lord and carried by the power of the Holy Ghost to the hearts of new missionaries who were there seeking direction from these living oracles. As the church grew, and as the call for more missionaries was answered, the force of missionaries as well as the number of missions grew rapidly. It became impractical for all missionaries to come to Salt Lake City; therefore a new and expanded facility needed to be built to receive the large number of wonderful young men and women who responded so favorably to a call from a prophet.

As the decades moved forward from those nascent efforts to train missionaries, the times and seasons dictated that changes should be made. As technology became more useful in our daily lives, and as secularism began to displace faith, two trends have been established in civil society today whose effects constrain our missionary efforts. These trends need to be considered by new missionaries as they enter the service of the Lord. First, society in general has moved beyond the traditional 1950's and early 1960's to the more raucous times of 1968 and the Vietnam War. This shift has resulted in a society that has endured the expanded use of drugs, a proliferation of sexual immorality, revolution, and a substitution of worldly success for transcendental certitude. All of which have focused the world's attention away from constants such as spiritual contentment, quietness, and stability (see Isaiah 32:17). Secularism has eroded many long held religious values and this phenomenon has moved like a tidal wave throughout both the church and the world. In a study done by David Voas, as reported in the Oxford Journals, published in the *European Sociological Review,* dated June 1, 2007, he found that, with respect to secularism and religion, the following applies:

> Although there are some minor differences in the speed of the decline (the most religious countries are changing more quickly than the least religious), the magnitude of the fall in religiosity during the last century has been remarkably constant across the continent. Despite these shifts in the prevalence of conventional Christian belief, practice and self identification, residual involvement [in religion] is considerable. Many people are neither regular churchgoers nor self consciously non religious. The term "fuzzy fidelity" describes this casual loyalty to tradition. Religion usually plays a minor role in the lives of such people. Religious change in European countries follows a common trajectory whereby fuzzy fidelity rises and then falls over a very extended period. The starting points are different across the continent, but the forces at work may be much the same.

Although his study confined itself to European countries, and while these conditions have not yet manifest themselves to this extent in the United States, the trend is clear and measurable.

The second condition that has manifested itself as part of this "fuzzy fidelity" is also a clear trend. Doctrinally, missionaries are less prepared to withstand the rigors of consecrated church service than they were in previous times. In times past, when church membership was smaller and when there were fewer missionaries, exposure to church doctrine, then as now, was part of the Sunday School curriculum. However, the immersion into doctrine was deep and meaningful in a day when the world moved at a slower pace. If there were deficiencies in preparation, this condition of doctrinal unpreparedness was taken care of in the Language Training Mission. Today, however, life's pace has accelerated and our youth have been pressured to "succeed" in a worldly sense beyond what could possibly have been conceived of back then. Those facing such pressures on time and resources do so amidst a tsunami of secularism that also is swamping our civil society with instant economic gratification. Unfortunately, we see the uneven success resulting from leaving the doctrinal preparation of our missionaries completely to the stakes and wards within the body of the church. In the Book of Mormon, this phenomenon is described by Jacob, as he quotes from the Zenos Allegory (Jacob 5:37), *"But behold, the wild branches have grown and have overrun the roots thereof; and because that the wild branches have overcome the roots thereof it hath brought forth much evil fruit; and because that it hath brought forth so much evil fruit thou beholdest that it beginneth to perish; and it will soon become ripened, that it may be cast into the fire, except we should do something for it to preserve it."*

I have seen this secularism take hold of the minds of younger generations throughout my teaching experience. I was a professor at the University of Utah for over 20 years, also an Institute teacher for ten of those years teaching courses on the Book of Mormon, the New Testament, including the Parables of Jesus and The Pearl of Great Price. Outside of my University and Institute role, I taught missionary preparation for over 20 years and had over 160 students in these missionary preparation courses. All of them were fine men, and the preparation we undertook there was to counter this secularism and the overzealous search for worldly success that has captured the imagination of many. In this missionary course, we attended to things of the soul, so that things of the self would not overpower the weightier matters of the gospel, namely the doctrine. The Savior warned His disciples in

Matthew 23:23 of this imbalance: *"Woe unto you, scribes and Pharisees, hypocrites! for ye pay tithe of mint and anise and cummin, and have omitted the weightier matters of the law, judgment, mercy, and faith:* ***these ought ye to have done, and not to leave the other undone.****"* This book has been written to assist missionaries in the preparation of their souls for the rigors of consecrated religious service to the nations of the world. This book is applicable to both sisters and brothers as they now embark on a meaningful journey in their service to the Lord. These eleven letters in Volume I are a result of questions regarding matters of the soul, sent to me by missionaries in the Missionary Training Center. It is hoped that the answers in my response will be regarded as "lessons that lead to a spiritual life" and fortify all who read them with a doctrinal foundation that will nourish the soul. It is with this in mind, so that the excellent preparation of the self, now found in the Missionary Training Centers of the world will bring forth the best fruit. If this balance between matters of the self and matters of the soul is achieved, the sweet fruit of the gospel will be available to those who will receive this good news by their efforts. It will also provide a buttress of doctrinal understanding against the onslaught of secularism and post modernity that will certainly assault them when they return.

In this day where all kinds of information are readily available, it is more important than ever to rank such information. All truth is not absolute, nor is all truth of equal value. There are yet too many casualties in the war for faith. This book seeks to restore that delicate balance between faith and reason that undergird our convictions in the reality of God's grace and mercy shown by revelation given to living prophets and apostles. The book will restore confidence in the absolute spiritual truth that provides a brilliant and compelling thread to the tapestry of ideas into which secularism must be placed. When faith is woven into this tapestry of ideas, a proper balance that reinstates faith and other absolute transcendental truths that once were self evident in our world can be struck. In an environment where science and empiricism have overpowered *a priori* transcendentalism, where science and relative truth masquerade as the only relevant truth, matters of the soul and its nourishment have become fundamental if such a balance between science and faith is to be restored.

William Hayes Pingree
Summer, 2014

LETTER ONE

PROLOGUE TO MISSIONARY SERVICE – WHY YOU HAVE BEEN CALLED

Dear Missionary,

You have qualified to receive a mission call and have begun to attend a missionary preparation course. I know you to be an intelligent young missionary who has prepared yourself through your schooling to embark upon what I will call one of the most important undertakings of your young life. I know you will ponder this letter carefully as it is an introduction to what you will learn. Its purpose is to set a broad framework for the doctrinal reasons why you have been led to accept such a calling. Sometimes, as we begin to understand our relationship to the church, we conflate worldly reasons for our service with spiritual reasons for building a life-long relationship with the Lord. We find that for a host of sophisticated reasons, we seek to be involved in missionary work. Many good-intentioned people have given us varied and different opinions as to why we should want to serve. These range from reasons such as enhancing our abilities in school to our ability to excel in church leadership after the mission. Organizational skills are touted, as they will be learned in the mission field and thus are invaluable to our future careers. We are counseled that we will learn to manage our time and thereby learn to apply these principles to our coming lives, which will be of incalculable value, as we become productive members of society.

This line of reasoning will layout many advantages with respect to skills you will acquire in the mission field. While these skills may indeed benefit you, they can miss the greater mark as to why you have been inspired to serve a mission. There are, in fact, better venues to learn these skills than the mission field. One could enroll in courses that teach such skills, and because these skills have intrinsic market value, such instruction would perhaps be more satisfactorily accomplished there. These skills are indeed by-products of missionary service, but when we try to seek out these kinds of reasons for serving the Lord, we are using a cost/benefit analysis, which in fact obscure the real reasons for our service. When such an analysis is undertaken, there is one common thread running through these reasons, and that is selfishness.

Missionary service is not a selfish endeavor and those who approach it as such will indeed eventually have to change their perspective, or the missionary experience shall invariably become a very unsatisfying one. One principle often left out is this: missionary work is **WORK**. Often in our world, young men and women have been exposed to such great electronic tools which are used to assist us in getting our work done, that we look to find ways to make our work easier. While this is good in some ways, we need to know before we serve a mission that it requires the ability to work and work hard. As President Monson has said ("Who Honors God, God Honors." *Ensign* November 1995, page 49), "Missionary work is HARD work. Missionary service is demanding and requires long hours of study and preparation that the missionary might match the divine message he proclaims. It is a labor of love, sacrifice, and devotion." These gifts indeed will be of incalculable value.

Further, as a mission is a very personal endeavor, it is important to acknowledge that many righteous individuals do not serve. There are great and inspired leaders, even some prophets who did not serve missions, and they did not go for a myriad of reasons. The reasons they did not serve dealt with military service, governmental restriction on the number of missionaries that could be called, and other valid, deeply personal reasons. None of these reasons dealt with selfish motives or goals. They were able to gain the knowledge and experience needed for their high calling because the Lord prepared them largely due to their honesty and selfless motives to serve. One thing you will learn in this preparation course is this: motive is everything. It is by this standard that you will come to know that the **most important convert you will ever make is you.** If your motives are not pure, personal conversion may be derailed and the great growth of your testimony could be imperiled.

By now, it must be very clear: missionary work is not about you and what you can receive from it. As Elder Boyd K. Packer has taught:

> The first great lesson is that this is not your mission – it is the Lord's mission. I know that we say 'I am going on my mission,' but it is not my mission, it is His mission...You will find through prayer, hard work, diligent study, and through the difficulties and disappointments you face that it is the Lord's mission. You will come to know that. ("What Every Missionary Should Know," page 2.)

Accordingly it is about the Lord and what He wants you to do to assist Him in bringing others to both understand His gospel and become prepared to receive His great gifts of salvation and exaltation. Correct preparation for such an undertaking as a mission will give you the doctrinal foundation and fortification so that your testimony will be girded with the certitude of redemptive faith required in the difficult and secular days that everyone knows lie ahead.

To be able to accomplish this great task, you must find the correct motive for service and then your efforts at preparation will find the best-intended results. The Lord will help all who seek to serve Him in the best possible way, but it is only when correct motive precedes preparation that the Lord will be able to aid you and help you develop great faith by study and by prayer. Reasons for serving a mission which are based upon self-interest are not virtuous reasons to serve. Albeit they may be advantageous to you, nonetheless they are not the best motivation for giving two years of your life to the Lord. You must also realize the fact that missionary work is hard work and will require a deep and abiding commitment on your part. This then points to the purpose of this long letter.

As you embrace the solemnity of a mission call and prepare to enter the mission field, it is a time for deep reflection, a time for the expression of gratitude, and a time to cultivate a deep sense of commitment. It is also a time to be happy, enjoy your family and friends and do things that will be of prodigious value to you in the coming years. While it is a time for great joy, it is not a time for needless frivolity; preparation awaits you so that your time will not be wasted. As we begin to seek out the doctrine of why you have been called as a missionary, the time for milk is over, it is a time to ponder and pray, it is time for meat! Why is this important? It is as Elder M. Russell Ballard said:

> When we are anchored to the great blessing of the Savior's life and Atonement, when our hearts are filled with gratitude to Him, we want to share our knowledge. And when we have our own internal knowledge of the doctrine, so deep and so strong, then we know that we can explain the gospel to anybody, anywhere, at any time and under any circumstances. That confidence comes from knowledge. (M. Russell Ballard's fireside talk on missionary work given at the University of Utah's Institute of Religion, October 15, 2006.)

As usual, the Book of Mormon gives us a point of departure early in its pages as to the doctrine of why you have been called. If we begin in Jacob 5, we find an allegory from the prophet Zenos about the House of Israel. He compares Israel to an olive tree with both wild and tame branches. An allegory is an extended metaphor, which means it can be compared to today's times and through it, we find relevance to your mission call. Relevance in our studies is vital. If you find our lessons not to be relevant, you must speak up, for if they are not relevant, they are not useful. Thus, motive is everything and relevance is the test to which your studies should be placed for them to be worthwhile.

This allegory was well known to Paul and understood as well by the apostles of New Testament times. He mentions the allegory in

Romans 11:16-20 and in verses 23-26. We read: *"For if the firstfruit be holy, the lump is also holy: and if the root be holy, so are the branches. And if some of the branches be broken off, and thou, being a wild olive tree, wert grafted in among them, and with them partakest of the root and fatness of the olive tree; Boast not against the branches. But if thou boast, thou bearest not the root, but the root thee. Thou wilt say then, The branches were broken off, that I might be grafted in. Well; because of unbelief they were broken off, and thou standest by faith. Be not highminded...And they also, if they abide not still in unbelief, shall be grafted in: for God is able to graft them in again. For if thou wert cut out of the olive tree which is wild by nature, and wert grafted contrary to nature into a good olive tree: how much more shall these, which be the natural branches, be grafted into their own olive tree? For I would not, brethren, that ye should be ignorant of this mystery, lest ye should be wise in your own conceits; that blindness in part is happened to Israel, until the fulness of the Gentiles be come in. And so all Israel shall be saved: as it is written, There shall come out of Sion the Deliverer, and shall turn away ungodliness from Jacob."*

What about all this talk about roots, branches and grafting? Paul understood it perfectly, but others, who lacked the Spirit of God, did not. Before the Bible was given to us today, it passed through the hands of such men who lacked spiritual understanding. The Bible is the word of God and it is mostly translated correctly; however, because some uninspired men omitted things they did not understand, the true meaning of the verses we read there is blurred. This fact then becomes "Exhibit A" as to why we need the Book of Mormon. Because, as Nephi taught, many plain and precious truths were taken away from the Bible, and the interpretation of Paul's words, as expressed by the allegory, have been lost and are not understood by today's Christian. Nephi told us (1 Nephi 13:26-27): *"And after they go forth by the hand of the twelve apostles of the Lamb, from the Jews unto the Gentiles, thou seest the formation of that great and abominable church, which is most abominable above all other churches; for behold, they have taken away from the gospel of the Lamb many parts which are plain and most precious; and also many covenants of the Lord have they taken away. And all this have they* done that they might pervert the right ways of the Lord, that they might blind the eyes and harden the hearts of the children of men." We will talk in detail about the "great and abominable church" when we discuss the Great Apostasy in Volume II, but suffice it to say here, that the great and abominable church is Babylon or the world. As we look around us today, the truth of this statement is self-evident.

Now, what do we learn from this allegory found in the Book of Mormon that not only clarifies Paul's words, but has relevance today to your call? First of all, the allegory was a scenario the Prophet Zenos used to describe events in the end-times concerning the House of Israel. The Lord made a covenant with Abraham that in his seed (his descendants) all nations of the earth would be blessed. In The Pearl of Great Price, Abraham 2:9-10 we read: *"And I will make of thee a great nation, and I will bless thee above measure, and make thy name great among all nations, and thou shall be a blessing unto thy seed after thee, that in their hands they shall bear this ministry and Priesthood unto all nations; And I will bless them through thy name; for as many as receive this Gospel shall be called after thy name, and shall be accounted thy seed, and shall rise up and bless thee, as their father."*

In the Book of Genesis we read concerning Abraham and Isaac. Abraham did not spare his son Isaac from sacrifice; however, the Lord did and because of Abraham's faithfulness, the Lord promised Abraham as follows in chapter 22:15-18: *"And the angel of the Lord called unto Abraham out of heaven the second time, And said, By myself have I sworn, saith the Lord, for because thou hast done this thing, and has not withheld thy son, thine only son: That in blessing I will bless thee, and in multiplying I will multiply thy seed as the stars of the heaven, and as the sand which is upon the sea shore...And in thy seed shall all the nations of the earth be blessed; because thou hast obeyed my voice."*

Of course, the son of Isaac was Jacob who wrestled with the Lord for this same blessing. His name was changed to Israel and through his twelve sons the blessings promised to Abraham were then delivered to the world. This is why in many patriarchal blessings (perhaps even in yours) the patriarch, in declaring lineage, will also tell the recipient that he or she is an heir to the blessings of Abraham, Isaac, and Jacob. Why is this so? Because in these three patriarch's descendants is the promise to Abraham fulfilled. This means that all who embrace the gospel of Jesus Christ are either a literal or an adopted son or daughter of the patriarchs and are part of the House of Israel. Zenos will place this fact into context for us. We understand that his allegory begins when Moses leaves Egypt and it is then that Zenos likens the House of Israel unto an olive tree. When the Lord led Israel out of Egypt, the tree had become old and had begun to decay. By bringing Israel out of Egypt, new and tender branches began to grow, but the main tree was still in decline and decay. These new and tender branches are the branches referred to as "tame".

Since the main tree remained in decline and was prone to apostasy, the Lord plucked off these new tame branches of the House of Israel and planted them all over His vineyard (which means the world) so that they would not die out even as the tree declined. As the decay of the old tree continued, the Lord hacked out the dying parts and they were burned. This has reference to the fact that the House of Israel wandered in the wilderness for forty years until all those that had demonstrated their unwillingness to listen to Moses had died. Remember, Moses was 80 years old when the exodus began and was 120 years old when the House of Israel entered into the Promised Land (see Exodus 7:7). The Lord continued to try to nourish the old tree, but inevitably, through the Babylonian captivity, the House of Israel was prone to decay, meaning apostasy.

Then the Lord grafted wild olive branches into the main tree. These wild olive branches were gentiles that received the promise of Abraham, and because they made covenants with the Lord (like baptism), they were grafted into the House of Israel. These wild olive branches were those spoken of by Peter and Paul in the Book of Acts; they revived the old tree even as the old branches lay in apostasy. In the Lord's time, both the wild and the revived branches were eventually scattered all over the world. Because these gentiles were grafted into the House of Israel, they brought forth tame fruit, not wild fruit. This means that they were heirs to the Kingdom of God because of being "adopted" into Abraham's house through Abraham's covenant.

The Lord then went into the world, His vineyard, to look for the tame branches from the House of Israel that he had planted all over the world. Since they were a literal part of the House of Israel, they too had brought forth much fruit. These would be the Nephites and others of whom we know not for we don't know where the Lord planted these living and tender branches of the House of Israel. We know of the Nephites because in 1 Nephi 15:12-13 tells us so: *"Behold, I say unto you, that the house of Israel was compared unto an olive tree, by the Spirit of the Lord which was in our father; and behold are we not broken off from the house of Israel, and are we not a branch of the house of Israel? And now, the thing which our father meaneth concerning the grafting in of the natural branches through the fulness of the Gentiles, is, that in the latter days, when our seed shall have dwindled in unbelief, yea, for the space of many years, and many generations after the Messiah shall be manifested in body unto the children of men, then shall the fulness of the gospel of the Messiah come unto the Gentiles, and from the Gentiles unto the remnant of our seed"* Suffice it to say, the Lord is looking for the tame fruit, those that would receive His ministry and His healing; in other words, those whom He could call His own.

The work of pruning, nourishing and tending the House of Israel continued for many generations. Those branches that did not bring forth good fruit were cast off. The main root of the tree remained nourished until verse 28 when the Lord explained that the end-times had come. One last time the Lord would go into His vineyard and make ready for the time when the seasons will come to an end. This is where you come in. The old tree had finally brought forth all kinds of wild fruit, meaning wild doctrines pertaining to the world, none of which was satisfactory. And so the Lord did, as Isaiah prophesied, bring forth a marvelous work and a wonder (see Isaiah 29) when he literally spoke to Joseph Smith. As Zenos had told us, the doctrines in these days were not good and so the Lord naturally told Joseph not to join any church because the fruit found there was not good. That does not mean that there were not many wonderful people in these churches, even among their leaders, for had not the Lord planted tame olive branches in the entire world? Not all of their doctrine was bad; some was good, just a little on the wild side!

As I said, here is where you come in. The servant of the Lord mentioned in the allegory is our Savior, the Lord Jesus Christ. You have been called to assist Him as the fellow servants spoken of in the allegory after verse 29, in the fullness of the times of the Gentiles (Paul's words, not mine). You are to be sent out by the Lord of the vineyard to gather all branches together and graft all of them back into the old olive tree known as the House of Israel. You have been or will be set apart under the authority of the Priesthood of God to bring these living members of the House of Israel home. Now the words of Paul referred to above in the book of Romans make perfect sense. Go back and read those verses cited above again and see if your understanding of his words has improved. Paul indeed knew exactly what he was talking about even if many of those who were not privy to the entire gospel did not.

The Book of Mormon in concert with the Bible presents a clearer picture of the true nature of the doctrines of the Lord. Our Heavenly Father knew, as shown by both Paul and Zenos, that the world would be a formidable and dangerous place in which to live. He knew that many would make unwise and disobedient choices, but because He loves all his children and has a plan for each of them, he taught us through this allegory that he would maximize His children's chances of being able to bear the tame fruit of redemption and salvation.

And now, because of what we have just learned, we can make three basic assumptions about you and your call. First, all of these things were understood from the beginning. As brethren, you were present and foreordained in the pre-mortal life to hold the Melchizedek Priesthood. Sisters, you also played an important role in our pre-mortal life, where your mission was not only explained, but also endowed with power. Second, you were reserved from the very beginning when our Father's plan began to be implemented to come to earth now, in the latter-days. Third, while in the aforementioned pre-mortal life, you were valiant enough to be able to be born in the covenant of that holy priesthood, or for those whose parents did not enter into the temple marriage covenant, to receive the promise that this blessing will one day come to you as you continue to faithfully exercise your faith. The Lord knew that things in these last days would be pretty mixed up. He knew that many who would have normally been able to be born in the covenant would not have the chance. You see, as we learned from Abraham's experience, the Lord delivers His blessings to His children by means of making covenants with His children under the authority of His priesthood. The first covenant then is baptism. The New Testament makes that abundantly clear (see Mark 16:16 and Acts 2:37-39). In both of these references, the Savior and then Peter were asked what was necessary to be able to come unto the Lord. Peter even expanded his answer to include the entire world, just as the Zenos' allegory teaches. Peter tells his audience (Acts 2:39), *"For the promise is unto you, and to your children, and to all that are afar off, even as many as the Lord our God will call."* This looks like "heavy grafting" to me and you are to be a big player in this as you accept your call. The grafting is accomplished through your preaching and teaching these truths to the people of the world. The mission field is indeed the world; the vineyard of the Lord, and the place to which you are called is your assignment in this great vineyard. The grafting occurs when people accept the graft by being baptized under the authority of the Priesthood of God.

    We will discuss the relevance of these assumptions as we move on in this letter. Suffice it to say, you were brought here because of your valiance, not because you have earned the right to go on a mission. When a friend of mine was called to be a stake president, Elder Boyd K. Packer reminded him that the "Lord could have chosen a fence post to lead this stake, but instead, He chose you." Never forget this lesson. Never forget that it is a humbling experience that requires a deeply personal commitment to be recommended and to be called on a mission. To that end, you must know that every man and woman who received a calling to minister to our Father's children received that calling in the councils of heaven before the world was (see *Teachings of the Prophet Joseph Smith*, page 365).

Some prophets have talked about receiving this calling. We read in the opening verses of the Book of Mormon of Lehi's vision. Because of this vision, Lehi took his family out of Jerusalem and because of this vision, he knew he was foreordained to do so. We read in Jeremiah 1:5, where the Lord told him, *"Before I formed thee in the belly I knew thee; and before thou camest forth out of the womb I sanctified thee...a prophet unto the nations."* Jeremiah knew that before he was born, the Lord had planned his mission. In Isaiah 6:8 the Lord tells him of his mission. It was again in the context of a grand council in heaven: *"Also I heard the voice of the Lord, saying, Whom shall I send, and who will go for us? Then said I, Here am I; send me."* Even the great Isaiah was told that he too was called to preach before he was sent to earth. How did Joseph Smith know that this was so? Well, he first came to know of the pre-mortal life when he was translating the Book of Mormon. In the translation process, he eventually came to Alma 13, where he first learned that there was a pre-mortal existence and in these verses he learned of the foreordination of men to minister to the earth and that all, including you, took an active part in these councils.

As Joseph learned of the pre-mortal existence, he became very curious about what went on while we dwelt there. His study prompted many questions. Answers came and are found in the Pearl of Great Price, the Doctrine and Covenants and other revelations Joseph received later in his life. But for our purposes, let's focus on Alma 13 and how it relates to you and your mission call. We learn in this particularly important chapter of the Book of Mormon those who were foreordained in the pre-mortal life to come here and fulfill the promise made by the Lord to His children as outlined in the Zenos allegory. In Alma 13:3 he tells us: *"And this is the manner after which they were ordained – being called and prepared from the foundation of the world according to the foreknowledge of God, on account of their exceeding faith and good works; in the first place being left to choose good or evil; therefore they having chosen good,* and exercising exceedingly great faith, are called with a holy calling...which was prepared with, and according to, a preparatory redemption for such."

This verse is talking about you. Why do I know this? Because you have prepared yourself "according to preparatory redemption" for such a mission, you were foreordained in the pre-mortal existence because of your exceedingly great faith in choosing good over evil. In the Doctrine and Covenants 138:53, we read of the leaders of this dispensation, *"The Prophet Joseph Smith, and my father, Hyrum Smith, Brigham Young, John Taylor, Wilford Woodruff, and other choice spirits who were reserved to come forth in the fulness of times to take part in laying the foundations of the great latter-day work."*

However, there were others, like you, who were also there. In verses 55-56, we read, *"I observed that they were also among the noble and great ones who were chosen in the beginning to be rulers in the Church of God. Even before they were born, they, with many others, received their first lessons in the world of spirits and were prepared to come forth in the due time of the Lord to labor in his vineyard for the salvation of the souls of men."* Let me emphasize that in the world of spirits, this was a preparatory calling, one which was extended there to be accepted and fulfilled here and because you had preparatory faith there, such faith that indicated to the Lord you had the potential to develop redemptive faith here.

Once that had happened, your preparation for this role began. Brethren, you were foreordained to hold the Melchizedek Priesthood and were endowed with power from on high. Sisters, although you do not hold the priesthood, you too were given priesthood power from on high to complete your important work. We know this is true because many of you were sent to parents who had married in the temple and therefore you were "born in the covenant." To those of you who were not "born in the covenant," once you accept this call, the Lord knows that as a consequence of your acceptance, He extended His promise to you that in a coming day these promised blessings and powers will be yours. Why is this important? Well, let's return to your patriarchal blessing.

This is what is meant by the words, "the blessings of Abraham, Isaac, and Jacob" that we discussed earlier. These are the fathers of the covenant of the gospel. They are the fathers of the House of Israel and it is to their seed that the allegory spoken by Zenos, the allegory of the Olive Tree has been given. It is to their descendants that the empowering blessings of the Lord are delivered to the children of our Heavenly Father. This means that the priesthood, the vehicle by which the blessings of salvation and exaltation are to be delivered to the House of Israel had to be given to you in a preparatory foreordained state. This would be done in the pre-mortal existence, as a promise to you that this very same priesthood, the actual power and authority of God would be given to you in your mortal existence to enable you to fulfill the mission you were given before the earth ever was. Sister missionaries were given the gifts to accomplish their missions through that same priesthood that would be on the earth at the time when the promises, detailed by Zenos, would be fulfilled. In other words, through this priesthood, along with its attendant ordinances, you would be authorized or allowed to do the things here on the earth that the Lord has asked you to do in our pre-mortal life.

If you were not commissioned and empowered by Him, the work you would try to do would have no validity in this world or the next one. We read in Doctrine and Covenants 50:13-14 and 17-18, *"Wherefore, I the Lord ask you this question – unto what were ye ordained? To preach my gospel by the Spirit, even the Comforter which was sent forth to teach the truth...Verily I say unto you, he that is ordained of me and sent forth to preach the word of truth by the Comforter, in the Spirit of truth, doth he preach it by the Spirit of truth or some other way? And if it be by some other way it is not of God."*

Even if you have prodigious gifts of persuasion, gifts of exposition, or the ability to highlight and teach great things, without His authority and authorization, it would not amount to anything. This ought to let you know that if it isn't the Lord's way, it doesn't matter much whose way it is. The gathering and grafting talked about by Zenos was done with the authorized servants of the Lord and they and they alone are able to do this great work. You have been called as one of those servants and hence, you have an awesome responsibility. We learned from Alma that many men and women were foreordained to come here at this time to recover the House of Israel. It was the Lord's plan that these wonderful men and women like you were either "born in the covenant" or were placed in a position to receive the gospel and its saving ordinances. The Zenos Allegory makes the reasons clear; you were given the wonderful opportunity to seek out and find those other magnificent people who have been prepared to be heirs of Abraham but for His purposes were planted "in the hithermost part of the Vineyard." You are called to rescue and retrieve them, and the Lord is anxious that you succeed for they are dear to Him.

The Lord has promised you the following (Doctrine and Covenants 4): *"Now behold, a marvelous work is about to come forth among the children of men. Therefore, O ye that embark in the service of God, see that ye serve him with all your heart, might, mind and strength, that ye may stand blameless before God at the last day. Therefore, if ye have desires to serve God ye are called to the work; For behold the field is white already to harvest; and lo, he that thrusteth in his sickle with his might, the same layeth up in store that he perisheth not, but bringeth salvation to his soul; And faith, hope, charity and love, with an eye single to the glory of God, qualify him for the work. Remember faith, virtue, knowledge, temperance, patience, brotherly kindness, godliness, charity, humility, diligence. Ask, and ye shall receive; knock, and it shall be opened unto you. Amen."*

Even in the very beginning of the restoration of the gospel, the Lord had Zenos' Allegory in mind. YOU are called to do His work, to go forth among the children of men into the Vineyard. YOU are called to nurture, prune and tend the olive tree, to recover the tame fruit and bring the branches back to the reinvigorated tree, the House of Israel. YOU have been empowered and clothed with great authority to bring the work, the work of reclamation and rescue, the very work in which God Himself has already invested thousands of years of His precious time to achieve.

He has given YOU the great honor to assist Him. We are now figuratively and actually back to the beginning. You see, my dear friend, you are the fulfillment of the promise given to all the families of the earth through Abraham. In Genesis 28:13-14, the Lord told Isaac, "*And, behold, the Lord stood above it, and said, I am the Lord God of Abraham thy father, and the God of Isaac: the land whereon thou liest, to thee will I give it, and to thy seed. And thy seed shall be as the dust of the earth, and thou shalt spread abroad to the west, and to the east, and to the north, and to the south* (even like unto an olive tree): **and in thee and in thy seed shall all the families of the earth be blessed.**" You, by virtue of being a member of the church and an heir to the blessings of Abraham are bringing the great message of Abraham, the gospel message that should the families of the earth embrace it, they too will be heirs to the Abrahamic covenant and promise.

Just as Nephi told his family (1 Nephi 15:14), "*And at that day shall the remnant of our seed know that they are of the house of Israel, and that they are the covenant people of the Lord; and then shall they know and come to the knowledge of their forefathers, and also to the knowledge of the gospel of their Redeemer, which was ministered unto their fathers by him; wherefore, they shall come to the knowledge of their Redeemer and the very points of his doctrine, that they may know how to come unto him and be saved.*" You are one that has been foreordained from the foundations of this very earth to be the Lord's messenger to bring the gospel of Abraham to those families. Whether they are Lamanites or Gentiles doesn't matter; it is to those families of the world you have been called by a prophet of God to fulfill another prophet's ancient promise long foreseen by our Lord. It is an honor that is almost too overwhelming to absorb, but try so to do. It is up to you to learn to love those whom you have been called to serve, just as the Lord Himself loves them. This will require diligence and great effort as you learn to selflessly commit yourself to His great work.

Now it is therefore a time of humility and a time to know that even in this great calling, the Lord desires you to consider yourself an unprofitable servant, even as did King Benjamin (Mosiah 2:21), "*I say unto you that if ye should serve him who has created you from the beginning, and is preserving you from day to day, by lending you breath, that ye may live and move and do according to your own will, and even supporting you from one moment to another – I say, if ye should serve him with all your whole souls yet ye would be unprofitable servants."* It is not a right or an entitlement to serve a mission, but it is a privilege for you have been called from the "weak" things of the earth (see 2 Corinthians 11:9). May you treat your call with the solemnity it deserves and commit, even today, to do all that is necessary to be prepared for the wonderful yet arduous task of serving the Lord. It will be my honor to assist you in the task of preparation so that your time in the Lord's Vineyard will be well spent.

With love, I remain your brother in the gospel,

LETTER TWO

PREPARATION: THE NEED TO BE WORTHY

Worthiness is an absolute requirement for missionary service, but the missionary needs to be able to distinguish between worthiness and having weaknesses.

Dear Missionary,

I certainly did enjoy reading your letter last week. You had just entered the Missionary Training Center and had been there for just a few days. I want to tell you that it is a very structured place and often because of this, things can be difficult. However, it seems you are doing well and this is good. Regarding languages, there have been many wonderful literary works and works of political philosophy written in both your native and foreign language. It is important to enhance your language skills irrespective of the language you will use to preach the gospel.

Your letter at one point turned to the subject of weaknesses and worthiness. You seemed to indicate that the two are related and if you just could overcome your weaknesses, you would feel more worthy to be on the mission. Both of these topics are important and often it is Lucifer who links them negatively. Worthiness is so very important because if a person is found unworthy to do the Lord's work, the Lord finds it difficult to fully accept the efforts of such a missionary; the hypocrisy is so evident, that He can't justify the actions of unworthy missionaries because if he did, He would be complicit in their actions. This is something that is impossible for God to do. Why? Because such behavior would allow mercy to rob justice, such an act would invalidate the Atonement.

That does not mean that worthy means perfect; on the contrary, worthiness shows to us the grace of Almighty God by giving us this most wonderful gift of repentance. Alma has much to say about this. It was this great prophet who was himself well acquainted with the issue of worthiness, as he explained to his son Corianton in Alma 40. Here he begins to lay the groundwork that will explain why worthiness, a part of the doctrine of justification, is extended as a gift to us through the grace of our Savior. In connection with this gift, he explains why this grace has been granted. In Alma 41:10-11, he explains, *"Do not suppose, because it has been spoken concerning restoration, that ye shall be restored from sin to happiness. Behold, I say unto you, wickedness was never happiness. And now, my son,* **all men** *that are in a state of nature, or I would say, in a carnal state, are in the gall of bitterness and in the bonds of iniquity; they are without God in the world, and they have gone contrary to the nature of God; therefore, they are in a state contrary to the nature of happiness."*

You see my dear friend, that if we aren't worthy, we are in a contrarian state, and in such a state, we cannot do the work of God because we would be asking the Lord to allow us to do His work without being able to have full access to His Spirit. In an unworthy condition, He cannot be as close to us as is required in this instance to do His work. All of us are imperfect, and likewise, all of us need repentance so that we can be cleansed from sin and the effects of living in this world; however, in order to be a special witness of His mission, we need to be worthy.

In Alma 42 we learn from his discussion with Corianton why this is so. After explaining the circumstances in the Garden of Eden on the subject of agency, in verse 4, Alma declares, *"And thus we see, that there was a time granted unto man to repent, yea, a probationary time, a time to repent and serve God."* You see my dearest friend from this very simple verse that repentance is a gift from God; it is by His grace that a time is granted to us so that we may repent and change. I can tell you that I have seen it among those who do not avail themselves of this time to change, that the Lord's Spirit is withdrawn, so that the desire to be clean is also lost. In Alma 12:11 we read, *"And they that will harden their hearts, to them is given the lesser portion of the word until they know nothing concerning his mysteries; and then they are taken captive by the devil, and led by his will down to destruction. Now this is what is meant by the chains of hell."*

When this happens, we begin to walk in darkness. So it is by the grace of God that a probationary time was granted unto man to repent. Sometimes, in our arrogance, we say we have our free agency to do anything we want. When we adopt this attitude, it eventually leads us to grief. Let's talk about some examples. First, in the Old Testament, we read during the time of Abraham of Sodom and Gomorrah. In Genesis 18, the Lord and Abraham have a discussion about this place. The Lord could not even find ten righteous souls there. Abraham asks the Lord in verse 32, *"And he said, Oh let not the Lord be angry, and I will speak yet but this once: Peradventure ten shall be found there. And he said, I will not destroy it for ten's sake."* But ten could not be found and we all know what happened to this place. The Lord had removed repentance as a gift to the people of Sodom and Gomorrah because they were not interested in repenting, and so they were destroyed.

A second example is found in the Book of Mormon. At the time the Nephite civilization went extinct, Mormon tells us why. In Mormon 1:13-14, said he, *"But wickedness did prevail upon the face of the whole land, insomuch that the Lord did take away his beloved disciples, and the work of miracles and of healing did cease because of the iniquity of the people. And there were **no gifts from the Lord, and the Holy Ghost did not come upon any, because of their wickedness and unbelief."*** Paul tells us in Ephesians 4:18-19, "Having the understanding darkened, being alienated from the life of God through the ignorance that is in them, because of the blindness of their heart: Who being **past feeling** have given themselves over unto lasciviousness, to work all uncleanness with greediness." In both of these cases, the Lord withdrew His Spirit and therefore no grace was extended to the people of Sodom or to the Nephites. They could not repent, and the Lord could not accept their efforts because they became rebellious and would not change. In Mormon 1:16 he tells us, *"And I did endeavor to preach unto this people, but my mouth was shut, and I was forbidden that I should preach unto them; for behold they had willfully rebelled against their God; and the beloved disciples were taken away out of the land, because of their iniquity."* There are occasionally times in the affairs of men when the Lord withdraws His Spirit and leaves us to our own devices. When this happens, the scriptures are filled with accounts of destruction and ruin that chronicle the withdrawal of His Spirit.

In these times, if we do not repent and accept His great gift of repentance and forgiveness, then great destruction comes into the world and people lose the ability to repent. We are perhaps far from these conditions, but how far, we don't know. Remember, the work is hard and this mission is not about you. It is about God's work and the people who in these days desperately need to hear His word. If they can't hear it because the Spirit cannot work with you due to unworthiness, then the purposes of God are thwarted. This He cannot allow. So while the **gift of repentance** is so readily available to us, we need to make sure that we avail ourselves of it so that we are *"clean that bear the vessels of the Lord"* (Doctrine and Covenants 38:42). Truly John explained to us in 1 John 1:6-7, *"If we say that we have fellowship with him, and walk in darkness, we lie, and do not the truth: But if we walk in the light, as he is in the light, we have fellowship one with another, and the blood of Jesus Christ his Son* ***cleanseth us from all sin."*** What a divine gift this gift of repentance is! It is granted to us because of the Lord's great love for us, and so it should not be feared, but embraced, even all the days of our lives. We don't just repent once, we repent every day and when necessary we allow the Lord's servants, His judges in Israel to assist us to return to His light.

In connection with the grace of repentance, there is another grace granted to us. This is the grace of probationary period. Without such a time, the gift of repentance would not have time to realize its full effect. This gift, granted to us by God, allows the grace of repentance the time necessary so that we might both learn from our mistakes and repent of our sins. If we mistakenly think we can just do as we please and then think afterwards we will not be held accountable, we are living in a fantasy world. Doctrine and Covenants 19:16-17 and 20 teaches us clearly, *"For behold, I, God, have suffered these things for all, that they might not suffer if they would repent; But if they would not repent they must suffer even as I...Wherefore, I command you again to repent, lest I humble you with my almighty power; and that you confess your sins, lest you suffer these punishments of which I have spoken, of which in the smallest, yea, even in the least degree you have tasted at the time I withdrew my Spirit."* All of us have sinned and all of us need to repent; the mission gives us an opportunity to use this greatest of gifts. So, if we have lied to our church leaders and not been "straight up" with them, then by default we are living in a parallel universe, one of rebellion. In such a state, we want the Lord to justify us in our sins, which, because of what we have read above, is impossible. Truly, as Amulek had previously taught Zeezrom (Alma 11:34), *"And Zeezrom said again: Shall he save his people in their sins? And Amulek answered and said unto him: I say unto you he shall not, for it is impossible for him to deny his word."*

    Now with this in mind, let's read on in Alma 42, his further counsel to Corianton. The entire chapter is very edifying, but let's focus on a few verses. In verses 15-17 we read, *"And now, the plan of mercy could not be brought about except an atonement should be made; therefore God himself atoneth for the sins of the world, to bring about the plan of mercy, to appease the demands of justice, that God might be a perfect, just God, and a merciful God also. Now, repentance could not come unto men except there were a punishment, which also was eternal as the life of the soul should be, affixed opposite to the plan of happiness, which was as eternal also as the life of the soul. Now, how could a man repent except he should sin? How could he sin if there was no law? How could there be a law save there was a punishment?"* There it is. Alma has laid things out very well. We have already discussed that we are saved by the grace of the gift of repentance. If there was no grace granted with its accompanying probation, then when we did something wrong we would immediately be punished according to the demands of the law; and there was a law given so that man might know what sin is.

As Nephi explained previously, and as we have discussed (2 Nephi 2:5), *"And men are instructed sufficiently that they know good from evil. And the law is given unto men. And by the law no flesh is justified; or, by the law men are cut off. Yea, by the temporal law they were cut off; and also, by the spiritual law they perish from that which is good, and become miserable forever."* Now we see more clearly the role of the law. It is not to save us, for law doesn't save. The Lord saves us from the effects of sin and from the effects of telestial life, including the effects of disease, weakness, and other proclivities of earth life. It is however, by the law that we come to know what the Lord expects of us; hopefully, our reaction to it leads us to Him.

It is the Lord that provides to us an escape from the effects of the law. This is done by His "condescension," the "stepping down" of the Son of God, to take upon Himself a mortal body so that He could also take upon Himself our sins as well as the effects of living in this world. This was explained carefully to Nephi (1 Nephi 11:16-17), *"And he said unto me: Knowest thou the condescension of God? And I said unto him: I know that he loveth his children; nevertheless, I do not know the meaning of all things."* Then the angel explained to Nephi what this was. Said he in verses 21 and 22, *"And the angel said unto me: Behold the Lamb of God, yea, even the Son of the Eternal Father! Knowest thou the meaning of the tree which thy father saw? And I answered him, saying: Yea, it is the love of God, which sheddeth itself abroad in the hearts of the children of men; wherefore, it is **the most desirable above all things.**"* Why? It is because, as Alma stated about his own experience with repentance, recorded in Alma 36:21 *"Yea, I say unto you, my son, that there could be nothing so exquisite and so bitter as were my pains. Yea, and again I say unto you, my son, that on the other hand, there can be nothing so exquisite and sweet as was my joy."* When we recognize the irreplaceable role of the Savior to cleanse us from our sins, and when we realize that without Him, the law of justice irrevocably will claim us, we know His love and approval is "the most desirable above all things."

Now my dear young missionary, we begin to see why we must be worthy. We can't be saved in our sins; the law, even strict obedience to the law, can't save us because it is not the law that saves us. It is the Son of God, the Lord Jesus Christ who condescended to do the will of His Father, to rescue us from sin. He was so moved by His love for His Father and His love for us that He, without being compelled to do so, came down and took on flesh; He suffered unimaginable agony and death for us as a ransom for our souls. It is through His love for us and because of His acceptance of us just as we are in our fallen state, and because He loves the Father perfectly, that He seeks for us a better life. He condescended to become mortal that we might escape death and the effects of mortality. Again, Amulek clearly spelled this out as we read in Alma 34:9-11, *"For it is expedient that an atonement should be made; for according to the great plan of the Eternal God there must be an atonement made, or else all mankind must unavoidably perish; yea, all are hardened; yea, all are fallen and are lost, and must perish except it be through the atonement which it is expedient should be made. For it is expedient that there should be a great and last sacrifice; yea, not a sacrifice of man, neither of beast, neither of any manner of fowl; for it shall not be a human sacrifice; but it must be* **an infinite and eternal sacrifice***. Now there is not any man that can sacrifice his own blood which will atone for the sins of another..."*

Because we cannot save ourselves and we cannot "earn" our salvation and exaltation through obedience, what then must we do to bring the atoning blood of the Savior upon us whereby we can **receive** His great gift? How do we accept this most desirable above all gifts? Alma tells us how in Alma 42:22-24, the great prophet explains, *"But there is a law given, and a punishment affixed, and a* **repentance** *granted; which repentance, mercy claimeth; otherwise, justice claimeth the creature and executeth the law, and the law inflicteth the punishment; if not so, the works of justice would be destroyed, and God would cease to be God. But God ceaseth not to be God, and mercy claimeth the penitent, and mercy cometh because of the atonement; and the atonement bringeth to pass the resurrection of the dead; and the resurrection of the dead bringeth back men into the* *presence of God; and thus they are restored into his presence, to be judged according to their works, according to the law and justice. For behold, justice exerciseth all his demands, and also mercy claimeth all which is her own; and thus, none but the truly penitent are saved."* Again, it is the Savior that does the work of salvation because of His Atonement; we receive the gift of salvation and exaltation as we become truly penitent.

When we have a broken heart and a contrite spirit, a subject that I never tire of discussing, we begin to ask, no, to beg as Alma did, for the blood of Christ to be applied to us. We begin to be so grateful for this great gift of repentance and forgiveness, that we will not cease wearying the Lord for its application. All of us who have come to know the Lord also have pleaded before Him for forgiveness and acceptance. In this act of contrition, we show our desire to accept the gift; and as we repent earnestly with "fear and trembling" before God as Alma himself did as recorded in Alma 36. As we try to retain the broken heart and contrite spirit so that we may be kept from further temptation, we are cleansed. Please take some time and read all of Alma 36 for it will give you perspective. Now, let's talk about weaknesses, for weakness is not sin. We all sin and we all have weaknesses. Let's begin again with the Apostle Paul. In 2 Corinthians 12:7 we read, *"And lest I should be exalted above measure through the abundance of the revelations, there was given to me a thorn in the flesh, the messenger of Satan to buffet me, lest I should be exalted above measure."* We see here that Paul himself had something that prevented him from being exalted above measure. Whatever this thorn was, it caused Paul to be humble and to glory in weakness. Moving on to verse 9 we read, *"And he said unto me, My grace is sufficient for thee: for my strength is made perfect in weakness. Most gladly therefore will I rather glory in my infirmities, that the power of Christ may rest upon me."* We all have some kind of "thorn" which reminds us that we are all children of the fall.

Notice, Paul says weakness, not weaknesses. This is important. The weakness (singular) that Paul is talking about is the result of the fall of Adam which has left us in our current condition of weakness. The brother of Jared explains it this way in his prayer to the Lord concerning the lighting of the vessels the Jaradites are to use to cross the ocean. In Ether 3:2, it is recorded that, *"O Lord, thou hast said that we must be encompassed about by the floods. Now behold, O Lord, and do not be angry with thy servant because of his weakness* [notice that the noun is singular, not plural] *before thee; for we know that thou art holy and dwellest in the heavens, and that we are unworthy before thee; because of the fall our natures have become evil continually; nevertheless, O Lord, thou hast given us a commandment that we must call upon thee, that from thee we may receive according to our desires."*

We see here there is a difference between the word "worthy" that we used above and general worthiness to which the brother of Jared refers. In a general sense, we are all unworthy, as the brother of Jared reasoned, because of the fall of man; in other words, we are unworthy because we have become telestial beings. As we noted earlier, "being worthy," means that we have repented of our sins; that we have realized we need the blood of Christ in our lives and have taken the appropriate steps, not covering or hiding our sins, to bring that about through accepting His great gift.

The above scripture, however, clearly defines the word "weakness" as meaning the conditions of the fall, conditions under which all of us are currently struggling. This condition of mortality makes us all in a general sense unworthy, but when we try to cover our sins and just do whatever it is we want, we are in a state of rebellion. This then makes us unworthy to receive the Spirit of the Lord and in that state He cannot justify us. Therein lies the difference between rebellious unworthiness and weakness. It shows that all of us have this weakness because all of us are products of the fall of man. There is no flesh on the earth that is not in a fallen state. This is often hard for us to accept. We are certain to admit to weaknesses, but to a condition of general weakness, about which we, in and of ourselves, can do nothing, it is hard to admit this condition to ourselves, let alone to others. We like to see ourselves as strong and powerful beings, in complete charge of all our affairs, including our salvation and exaltation; we have a hard time admitting that we can't bring our own salvation into effect. It comes to us SOLELY as a gift, based on a broken heart and a contrite spirit as we seek the favor of our Lord, which favor He is very willing to grant us, upon our being meek and penitent. As Lehi taught Jacob, in 2 Nephi 2:3, *"...Wherefore, I know that thou art redeemed,* [not because of your hard works, Jacob, we might add, but] *because of the righteousness of thy Redeemer..."* Some of us may often feel that if we will simply work harder and show the Lord we are strong, we will overcome this weakness. When asked about the Lord's role in this, we quickly add, "Of course, with His help." The words of Lehi truly contradict such sentiment, and put such mawkishness to route. Such thoughts are folly.

The Lord went on to tell us, with respect to spiritual weakness, as well as other weaknesses that pertain to our fallen state, in Ether 12:27, *"And if men come unto me I will show unto them their weakness. I give unto men weakness that they may be humble; and my grace is sufficient for all men that humble themselves before me; for if they humble themselves before me, and have* **faith** *in me, then will I make weak things become strong unto them."* Notice what the Lord has told us. First, He tells us that He gives us "weakness," not weaknesses, and second, this weakness is to be overcome by faith, not independently by our own works. While it is true that our weaknesses grow out of the weakness that is mortality, without His help, obtained through our faith, the condition of mortality known as weakness, is not overcome, despite all our works. Good works, which are evidence of faith, follow faith; they do not precede it.

What I want you to see, my friend, is that all of us have some condition, either spiritual, physical or both which is a manifestation of the weakness of our mortality and of the condition described as the fall of man. A condition I might add that is absolutely necessary for our progression. The primary reason for this condition, as we learn in the temple, is that a Savior is to be provided for us that will enable us to return to the Lord's presence. What am I saying with all of this? It is important to view any physical disability as a tutorial the Lord has given us to remind us of the telestial and imperfect state in which we now live. Because of this condition of telestial weakness and to help us remember to call upon the name of the Lord (see

Doctrine and Covenants 19:28) we seek not only His help, but His strength as well. We must always remember that it is in His strength, not ours, that our salvation and exaltation is made sure. Therefore, if we think it is weakness not to take medicine, or to allow others to help us, we have need of repentance and change; by not relying on the things the Lord has given us to make us well, we mock and tell Him we are stronger than we really are. He will help us if we are certain to rely on Him. We learn in 2 Nephi 31: 19, "*...for ye have not come thus far save it were by the word of Christ with unshaken faith in him, relying WHOLLY upon the merits of him who is mighty to save.*" Accordingly, regarding both physical and spiritual weakness, we must of course, follow His counsel in faith, as He directs us through the Spirit to the things we must do.

    Now that we know the difference between being worthy and having weakness even though weakness often leads to sin, it doesn't necessarily have to. In fact, realizing we have weaknesses should allow us to rely on the Savior and His Atonement to lift us up, away from our weaknesses. Since weakness and worthiness are often linked, they need to be separated but not disassociated. I am glad that you were one that was completely open and honest with your church leaders, but because weakness and worthiness are still associated together in our minds, let's look directly at both of these together and see how they relate one to another. When we feel weak, sometimes we feel unworthy. It would not be amiss to speak to your mission president, but if you have been "straight up" with your church leaders who recommended you for this mission, I would have you consider the counsel of Elder Marvin J. Ashton, then of the Council of the Twelve. In a General Conference address as reflected in his book, *The Measure of our Hearts,* Elder Ashton explains how worthiness and weakness are interrelated. He draws a distinction between the two that is important for us to consider. In the chapter entitled, "I Would be Worthy," he clarifies the difference:

> In recent weeks I have had some conversations that have made me ponder the meaning of the word "worthy." As I talked to a twenty-year old man, I discussed his attitude about going on a mission. He said, "I wanted to go, but I'm

not worthy." "Who made that judgment?" I asked. "I did," was his answer. On another occasion I asked a young lady who was contemplating marriage if she was going to the temple. She said, "I'd like to, but I am not worthy." In response to the same question of who determined her unworthiness, she too said, "I did."

...Each of these people seemed to have made his or her own determination about worthiness. We do not have to be hindered by self-judgment. All of us have the benefit and added wisdom of a bishop and a stake president to help us determine our worthiness and, if necessary, to assist us in beginning the process of becoming worthy to accomplish whatever goal we wish to achieve. When we take it upon ourselves to pass self-judgment and simply declare, "I'm not worthy," **we build a barrier to progress and erect blockades that prevent our moving forward.** We are not being fair when we judge ourselves. A second and third opinion will **always** be helpful and proper. It occurs to me that many do not understand what worthiness is. Worthiness is a process, while perfection is an eternal trek. We can be worthy to enjoy certain privileges without being perfect. (Conference Report, April, 1989.)

It seems that Brother Ashton has counseled us not to engage in self-judgment without the benefit of others. He declares to us that worthiness is a process and if we engage in needless self-judgment, then we will build barriers to our own spiritual progress. Of course you have weakness, it is part of being mortal. But, you have been interviewed by men who have been appointed by the Lord to be "Judges in Israel," men who have the keys to judge worthiness. When your stake president laid his hands on your head, he pronounced by the authority of the priesthood and in the name of the Lord that you are worthy in every way. He knew you were "straight up" with him and you were. Don't let these feelings of unworthiness enter your mind just because you have weakness. These weaknesses are given to us as part of our mortal probation and they will indeed lead us to our Savior and to contrition of our hearts; this means we must rely on Him by acknowledging our weaknesses and seeking for His help in rising above them. When we feel unworthy because of weakness, please know that these feelings come from an alien source, a stranger to our welfare, even Lucifer who is neither competent nor unbiased in rendering such a judgment. You have been honest about your life and as it is with all of us, as we learn to repent, we become worthy.

So we have weaknesses; in them we must learn to trust the Savior, for it is He who understands that weakness is part of mortality and it was He who gave His life so that you and I may overcome them. It is also He that has paid the price for your sins and for mine. Would it not be blasphemous if we were to reject His healing blood when He and His servants have declared you worthy? With respect to weaknesses and worthiness, Elder Ashton continues:

> When we dwell on our own weaknesses, it is easy to dwell on feeling that we are unworthy. Somehow we need to bridge the gap between continually striving to improve and yet not feeling defeated when our actions aren't perfect all the time. We need to remove "unworthy" from our vocabulary and replace it with "hope" and "work." This we can do if we turn to quieter, deeper, surer guidelines – the words of our prophets and leaders, past and present. (Conference Report, April, 1989.)

Another one of these prophet leaders, President George Q. Cannon said some beautiful things about our feelings and about how the Lord feels about us. Early in the twentieth century, he declared:

> Now, this is the truth. We humble people, we who feel ourselves sometimes so worthless, so good-for-nothing; we are not so worthless as we think. There is not one of us but what God's love has been expended upon. There is not one of us that He has not cared for and caressed. There is not one of us that He has not desired to save and that He has not devised means to save. There is not one of us that He has not given His angels charge concerning. We may be insignificant and contemptible in our own eyes and in the eyes of others, but the truth remains that we are children of God and that He has actually given His angels...charge concerning us, and they watch over us and have us in their keeping. (*Gospel Truths*, pages 3-4.)

I think it is really important to realize that when we have been declared worthy, and when we have disclosed all to our bishop or stake president, then we are worthy irrespective of the feelings Lucifer may place within our hearts. Brother Cannon's words have brought me great comfort over the years and I would hope you would always remember that indeed angels are watching over you and that the Lord loves you and cares for you more than you will ever know. It is well to remember the words of Shakespeare, in his play "Measure for Measure." Here he counsels us, "Our doubts are traitors, and make us lose the good we oft might win by fearing to attempt." (Act 1, scene 4, lines 77-79.) Don't let any doubts of your worthiness enter in for they are indeed traitors and will prevent you from doing the good the Lord intends. If you remain humble, and glory in weakness as did the Apostle Paul, you will find yourself stretched and drawn to greater heights and to greater growth than you have yet experienced. Cast that burden onto the Lord and "bear a song away." As you do, your confidence in Him will grow, you will come to know Him as the "author and finisher of our faith." You will be blessed with peace and find your faith unshakeable. Take care of yourself, and know that the things in this letter are there to provide comfort and hope.

With the best and deepest regards for you and your well-being,

LETTER THREE

THE FIRST LESSON OF SUCCESSFUL MISSIONARY SERVICE

The ability to learn by the Spirit is the most important lesson a missionary can acquire. It is the foundation of a successful missionary experience.

Dear Missionary:

You mentioned that the adjustment to the Missionary Training Center was kind of different. I do get this response from many missionaries because no one can know how the MTC will affect him or her until he or she actually gets there. Many missionaries find the environment to their liking and others find it to be an adjustment. The MTC has a wonderful spirit about it, but because it is not like the environment you just left, it sometimes seems that it has the spirit of "boot camp" about it. This is to be expected. I have often asked, how else does one take so many missionaries with such varied spiritual, economic, social and educational backgrounds and do what is necessary to prepare them for actual missionary service? There really is no other way. So, I am glad you have adjusted and are doing well. For others, it may take a little time, but the benefits of preparation under such circumstances are great and they too will come to appreciate the Missionary Training Center.

I read your letter with great interest especially as it related to teaching by the Spirit. You have described the process very well. I have tried to do this my entire life since I was in the mission field. I can tell you that your experience of being blessed every time you leave your comfort zone, or risk yourself to become vulnerable to the Spirit, is one that will continue throughout your life. For example even though I knew by my own experience what your needs in the mission field would be and had appropriately prepared my letters to you, sometimes I felt the Spirit often intercede and direct the letter to more pressing points that needed to be made. The Spirit often moved my thoughts to areas that were not planned but nonetheless were vital for the letter. This ought to tell you my dear friend, how much the Lord loves you and how much He wants you to succeed. Each mission is unique and the Lord has called you to a wonderful place, and He expects you to teach by the Spirit. Although the people you are called to teach live a long way from home, even still, if you had been called to a closer venue, the same lesson here would apply. The Spirit does strive with many in that far away place, but to have an ordained minister of the gospel of Jesus Christ in their midst is a new thing for many of them. As you enhance your ability to follow the promptings of the Spirit, you will be led on a wonderful journey that will teach you things that you will use for the rest of your life.

Some family or person there in that place was specifically being readied and strengthened to hear the Gospel by your own mouth and was being fortified to accept it. There are people now looking for you. You might even have some of them say to you, "I had a dream in which I saw you." Such experiences are usually less spectacular, but I know you see that many may feel that they recognized you when you came in contact with them. It will be an awesome experience, so please let me know when this happens. In that light, there are a few things I want to talk to you about. I want you to know that you are experiencing the Spirit in a new and correct way. **Learning to follow the Spirit the correct way,** meaning bringing forth a broken heart and a contrite spirit, is the first and most important lesson you can learn at the Missionary Training Center. What does this mean? Elder Bruce D. Porter, in his conference address in October 2007 gave us a very good definition ("A Broken Heart and a Contrite Spirit," Conference Report 2007, page 31). "Those who have a broken heart and a contrite spirit are willing to do anything and everything God asks of them." When we are **willing** to do what the Lord wants of us, not that we always are able, we become meek and teachable. The operative word is "willing." To this point, the Lord told the brethren in Kirtland, in Doctrine and Covenants 64:34, *"Behold, the Lord requireth the heart and a willing mind..."* So, in this context, we do not desire to "impress" the Lord with our obedience, in the sense that we seek to earn blessings. No, our obedience for us now becomes sacred and held closely between the Lord and ourselves; it is not for public consumption. Because we have brought forth such a sacrifice, we have learned to rely on the Lord and to go quietly about His business, even as an unprofitable servant (see Mosiah 2:21).

Rudyard Kipling wrote of a broken heart and a contrite spirit back in 1897 when he penned these in his poem, "Recessional":

> The tumult and the shouting dies;
> The captain and the kings depart;
> Still stands thine ancient sacrifice,
> An humble and a contrite heart.

The Savior Himself possessed the ultimate broken heart and as a result, performed the ultimate sacrifice that He and He alone could make, as He died on Calvary. His will was completely swallowed up in the will of the Father and in that manner of complete surrender to the Father's will; quietly He brought forth that sacrifice of sacrifices that redeemed all men. This is the example He wishes us to follow. Not one that is spectacular, for His sacrifice was made at a small place called Judea. Josephus, the great Jewish and Roman historian, is the only intellectual that even noted our Savior's existence and then only briefly. These sacrifices, of a broken heart and a contrite spirit, like that of the Savior, are not ones that call attention to ourselves, but are worked out quietly and privately in that great Gethsemane known only to you and found only in your own heart.

Thus, the subject of this letter and one that will be repeated frequently in my letters to you is the need for a broken heart and a contrite spirit. Why? Because it is at the core of the Savior's very example of how He served others; even by the ultimate sacrifice of His precious life. Once you come to understand its importance, you will find references to the broken heart and the contrite spirit everywhere in the scriptures. Why? It is because without it, we cannot have sufficient faith to do the work of the Lord correctly. Without these attributes, the works we try to do will be done without faith and therefore they may be haphazardly done. Certainly we run the risk of having such efforts fail to bring the appropriate approval of our Heavenly Father. There are some who do not learn this lesson. So, trying to respond to your question about how we bring this about, I have thought long and hard about all of this and would like to begin with you in Doctrine and Covenants 39.

This is the section for skeptics and cynics, people who often think that their own views are superior to that of the Lord. I sometimes fall into this category, as do many who are very educated and, who, quite frankly, think too much about certain things. These same individuals allow what the Lord has said about them to become parsed and therefore less relevant. And so with that in mind, I have found the counsel given here to be particularly appropriate to myself and I hope to you. In verses 8-12 we read, *"And verily I say unto thee, thine heart is now right before me at this time; and, behold, I have bestowed great blessings upon thy head; Nevertheless, thou hast seen great sorrow, for thou has rejected me many times because of pride and the cares of the world. But, behold, the days of thy deliverance are come, if thou wilt hearken to my voice, which saith unto thee: Arise and be baptized, and wash away your sins, calling on my name, and you shall receive my Spirit, and a blessing so great as you have never known. And if thou do this, I have prepared thee for a greater work. Thou shalt preach the fulness of my gospel, which I have sent forth in these last days, the covenant which I have sent forth to recover my people, which are of the house of Israel. And it shall come to pass that power shall rest upon thee; thou shalt have great faith, and I will be with thee and go before thy face."*

Now, I know that the above scripture tells James Covill (an early member of the church) that he needs to be baptized because his heart is now right before God. Thus, he now meets the conditions for baptism found in Doctrine and Covenants 20:37, *"And again, by way of commandment to the church concerning the manner of baptism - All those who humble themselves before God, and desire to be baptized, and come forth with **broken hearts and contrite spirits**, and witness before the church that they have truly repented of all their sins, and are **willing** to take upon them the name of Jesus Christ...shall be received by baptism into his church."* There it is again! A broken heart and a contrite spirit! The Lord makes this abundantly clear: without a broken heart and a contrite spirit, we can't really enjoy an abundance of His spirit. Truly the broken heart and the contrite spirit are elemental components of faith. If we are not possessed with them, we often reject Him because of the pride of the world.

However, if we now realize that our hearts are prepared to receive His Spirit, then we can trust Him and feel His Spirit in a greater measure. How do we do this, you may ask? Well, the Doctrine and Covenants provides the answer. In Section 50:10-12 we read, *"And now come, saith the Lord, by the Spirit, unto the elders of his church, and let us reason together, that ye may understand; Let us reason even as a man reasoneth one with another face to face. Now, when a man reasoneth he is understood of man...even so will I, the Lord, reason with you that you may understand."* The Lord will reason with us, if, as Section 39:8-10 requires, *"Thine heart is now right before me at this time...behold, the days of they deliverance are come."* This means that when we have a broken heart and a contrite spirit (the true meaning of having our hearts right before Him), He will now reason with us that we may understand in a greater context the events in our life and the vicissitudes and trials as well as the triumphs and joys. He will reason with us. It is in reasoning, if you will, that we gain perspective and learn of His thoughts. We are seasoned through reasoning with Him for it is ordained of God if such reasoning is preceded by faith.

How does this reasoning work? How do we reason with the Lord? To begin to answer this question, let's look to Section 6 of the Doctrine and Covenants. We read of the Lord's answer to Oliver Cowdery about how His Spirit works as follows in verses 14-15, *"Verily, verily, I say unto thee, blessed art thou for what thou hast* done; *for thou hast inquired of me, and behold, as often as thou hast inquired thou hast received instruction of my Spirit. If it had not been so, thou wouldst not have come to the place where thou art at this time. Behold, thou knowest that thou hast inquired of me and I did* **enlighten thy mind**; *and now I tell thee these things that thou mayest know that thou hast been enlightened by the Spirit of truth."* Here we see, that as we reason with Him, in faith, we begin to understand and feel His Spirit. He told Oliver Cowdery here that when He speaks to him, such conversations **enlighten** his mind and Oliver will think things and understand things previously not thought nor understood. With this experience, often a "burning" within happens or a feeling of love and gratitude for God will accompany this experience. I can honestly say that this does not happen all of the time, but if our hearts are right and broken, what does always happen is enlightenment. It happens as we grow in the truth of His word. The emotional feelings that are most present for me are feelings of confidence, peace and determination to follow the greater knowledge (the ah-hah, if you will) that I have just received.

    When we think or reason with God, we are often drawn to the times when the Lord or His prophets have performed great works or miracles. Often, we come to expect too much and when this does not happen, we become discouraged and cease trying to reason with Him. Let's consider this response and see why we must indeed continue in prayer. As Elijah taught us in 1 Kings 19, verses 11 and 12, we read, *"And he said, Go forth, and stand upon the mount before the LORD. And, behold the LORD passed by, and a great and strong wind rent the mountains, and brake in pieces the rocks before the LORD; but the LORD was not in the wind: and after the wind an earthquake; but the LORD was not in the earthquake: and after the earthquake a fire; but the LORD was not in the fire: and after the fire a* **still small voice**.*"* This still small voice does not always produce great physical manifestations of spiritual outpourings; nevertheless, it is the word of God to us and we must be able to have our hearts right to hear it. Our hearts are right if we are not filled with pride and seek to do God's will with a love for God's work. Mother Teresa once said (and I love this quote), "There are few great events in life that will define greatness; only small events done with a great amount of love" (see *Mother Teresa – Come Be My Light, pages 267-293).* When we adopt this attitude, our hearts are right before our Heavenly Father.

When we understand that the Spirit is in the still small voice, we begin to seek for it. Many missionaries confuse emotion with the Spirit. The Spirit comes with this "still small voice" and it can produce an emotional response; but **more often and more predictably,** it comes with the feelings of peace and strength, not crying or emoting, although this can and does happen. If it seems that we are over emotional, we are putting our desires before His and are not "waiting upon the Lord," something that is absolutely required when doing missionary work. We will address this subject later in this letter. When we begin to seek after the still small voice, we begin to see things differently; we begin to have elevated thoughts as we contemplate His great work. We find ourselves steeped in patience and understanding with a desire to seek additional knowledge. We don't expect great manifestations, but instead we look for and expect regular communication. When this happens, we then know that the Spirit of the Lord is with us; we feel His pleasure at our actions and thus we know we are justified before Him (see Mosiah 4:8-12). President Spencer W. Kimball, in the first area conference of his presidency held in Germany, France and Holland in 1976, explained:

> The burning bushes, the smoking mountains...the Cumorahs and the Kirtlands were realities but they were the exceptions. The great volume of revelation comes...in the less spectacular way – that of deep impressions without spectacle or dramatic events. Always expecting the spectacular, many will surely **miss** entirely the constant flow of communication (European Area Conference, August 1976).

I know that there are a few missionaries in the field that seem to have fantastic spiritual experiences, loaded with exaggerated emotion, where they tell us about great spiritual manifestations or about visions they perhaps have seen. It has been my experience, however, even knowing these things are possible, that when such things do happen, those to whom they happen are often very circumspect about them; they hold them sacred and are loath to discuss them. As the Lord states in D&C 63:64 *"Remember that that which cometh from above is sacred, and must be spoken with care, and by constraint of the Spirit."* Elder Boyd K. Packer stated:

> Dreams, visions and visitations are not uncommon in the Church in this dispensation. It may be that you will be the recipient of a marvelous spiritual experience. I have come to know that these experiences are personal...Ponder them in your heart and do not talk lightly about them [see Alma 12:9]. ("The Things of the Soul," CES Fireside, November 7, 1993.)

When such grand experiences are shared, they may be true, and because there is no way that we can verify such experiences, I thus caution you, my friend, to be careful of these. I truly believe that angels do watch over missionaries and sometimes, these angels are even seen by the missionaries; however, in zeal that precedes knowledge (unfortunately) there are some missionaries that "push the envelope" as it were. You have probably noticed some missionaries that exhibit much pride in themselves and their spiritual proclivities and this fact shows up in their testimonies. They often relate these "exaggerated" spiritual experiences, which may leave us feeling uncomfortable or even in a state of disbelief. You must be prudent about such things. As I said, angels do watch over missionaries and there are deep emotional as well as spiritual experiences, but more often the Spirit is manifest to us in quiet ways. And it is these quiet expressions that leave our spirits tutored and strengthened.

Some may ask, is it appropriate to see the angels or have these seemingly extra-spiritual experiences? I think the answer to the question lies in looking at the Lord's Prayer. In Matthew 6:8-13, we read: *"Be not ye therefore like unto them: for your Father knoweth what things ye have need of,* **before** *ye ask him. After this manner, therefore pray ye: Our Father which art in heaven, Hallowed be thy name. Thy kingdom come. Thy will be done in earth, as it is in heaven.*

Give us this day our daily bread. And forgive us our debts, as we forgive our debtors. And lead us not into temptation, but deliver us from evil: For thine is the kingdom, and the power, and the glory, for ever. Amen." We see here that when we are on the Lord's agenda, we consistently, even daily, ask Him for our bread and breath. He has knowledge of what we need before we ask Him. If we need to see these angels, or have unusually dramatic spiritual experiences, we will. Is it appropriate to ask to see angels or ask for these kinds of experiences? These kinds of experiences are not to be sought after or to be misread. We are not necessarily "more" faithful if we see the angels than those that do not. If angels are required, and if we have faith, we will see them because we receive the prompting to ask to see them. There are many of the Brethren who certainly have enough faith to see angels, but the situation does not require their presence, therefore, they don't ask (see Doctrine and Covenants 88:63-65).

If it is not required, and they then seek a more profound witness, they would in effect, be tempting God. This then would be a sin. If the Lord prompts you to fast and to pray to see these angels, He will do so by reasoning with you. He generally does not require that you so ask, and so, if that is His desire, not yours, you will also see them. However, it is not very likely that He will do so because you know that they are there and He knows that you know this, and unless it serves a purpose known only to Him, chances are you will not see them. You have important knowledge to gain; knowledge that has been ordained to be taught you through the MTC experience. That too, is of the Lord.

So I am happy that you are finding contentment at the MTC. It can be a place of spiritual tension as well as one of tranquility. I know that many missionaries feel that they need to demonstrate their spirituality even to the extent that they exceed their own spiritual abilities. Over time, however, most of them will calm down and realize that we are not interested in spectacular divine manifestations. If they come, they come at the behest of the Lord; if they do not, we trust in the Lord and follow, as did Elijah, the promptings of the Holy Ghost. It is important to remember the response the Prophet Joseph Smith gave to

President Martin Van Buren, as recorded by Elias Higbee:

> In our interview with the President, he interrogated us wherein we differed in our religion from the other religions of the day. Brother Joseph said we differed in mode of baptism, and the gift of the Holy Ghost by the laying on of hands. We considered that **all other considerations were contained in the gift of the Holy Ghost,** and we deemed it unnecessary to make many words preaching the Gospel to him... (see *History of the Church of Jesus Christ of Latter-day Saints, Volume IV, page 42.)*

From the above, it is clear that the Prophet Joseph Smith followed in the same manner as Elijah did. The great difference between members of the Church of Jesus Christ of Latter-day Saints and others is we enjoy a fullness of the gift of the Holy Ghost. We do not need exaggerated and often untrue public expressions of our missionary tools. We can possess a full manifestation of the power of the Spirit when the Spirit enlightens our minds or bears testimony of the truth to our hearts (see Doctrine and Covenants 6:14-15). It is sensitive and not to be taken for granted. It is given to us as we bring forth the broken heart and the contrite spirit along with that sighted faith that is required to do missionary work. The quiet gift of the Holy Ghost supersedes all other manifestations, especially if they are pompous and are expressed for the purpose of making it seem we are more spiritual than others. We must remember the Gift of the Holy Ghost comes to us in rich abundance if our hearts are right and broken before God. President Joseph Fielding Smith has written:

> A manifestation of an angel would not leave the impression as firmly as if we receive truth by the power of the Holy Ghost. Personal visitations might become dim as times goes on, but this guidance of the Holy Ghost is renewed and continued day after day, year by year, if we live worthy of it. (*Doctrines of Salvation, Volume I, page 44.)*

We see, then, that President Smith's counsel to us is so true and is right in line with what the Prophet Joseph Smith said to us earlier. We have the Holy Ghost. Unlike angels, the Holy Ghost is Deity and it is the right of every worthy member of the church to receive revelation and promptings by the presence of the Spirit. This is the very core of why you have been called and why this work is not about you. President Smith further elaborated on this message:

> Every soul upon the face of the earth who has a desire to know it [the gospel] has the privilege, for every soul that will humble himself, and in the depths of humility and faith, with a contrite spirit, go before the Lord, will receive that knowledge just as surely as he lives. ("A Testimony of Truth," Conference Report, October 1949, pages 87-90.)

Therefore, in connection to the most important lesson stated above, it is vital that **we cultivate our ability to feel the Spirit and to understand what promptings are of the Spirit. It is to be longsuffering, meek, and humble so as to enhance our ability to receive Him.** I know that this is not always the most spectacular way to learn truth, but it is the most sure. Evidence of angels, visions and revelations and even miracles come to us because the Holy Ghost is with us. To receive such manifestations, which may be nice, are however, by definition, **inferior** ways to know the truth. The best way is by the power of the Holy Ghost, and for that, we need a broken heart and a contrite spirit.

What we learn here is very important. When it comes to knowing the truth, the Lord does not generally deal with huge and very loud, epic "Hollywood-like" productions. He can and often is grand and great in the manifestation of His power, but more often than not, to those He loves, it is done by small means, even a still, small voice. We read in Alma 37:6-7, *"Now ye may suppose that this is foolishness in me; but behold I say unto you, that by small and simple things are great things brought to pass; and small means in many instances doth confound the wise. And the Lord God doth work by means to bring about his great and eternal purposes; and by very small means the Lord doth confound the wise and bringeth about the salvation of many souls."* As a result of small things, great things will become a self-evident truth. As we attend to the small things, like reading our scriptures and taking time to ponder and pray, we will find spiritual "ah-hah's" and our confidence in the Lord will grow.

Now that you have entered the Missionary Training Center, it will afford you the ability to overcome obstacles. The first and most important lesson, learning by the Spirit, will at the same time help you to master the ability to seek the Spirit. You will do so in a way that allows the Lord Himself to bring to pass His work through you while you are on this mission. You must never cultivate a rebellious spirit, or one that is ripe for a fight. Contention is not of God (see Mosiah 2:32-33) for you must learn to reason with Him, not to argue with Him; learn His ways, the **only** way to do this is by bringing forth a sacrifice of a broken heart and a contrite spirit. An angry and rebellious spirit is counter to a broken heart and a contrite spirit. With that in mind, you will come to trust the Lord and rely on His marvelous ways. In the beginning, it is often hard to see this; you have been through so much training, and you will go through a lot more, so that we think our spirit has been so engineered to respond to our calling in a certain manner. We often think that process over substance will bring us the best results. It is true that we learn many processes in becoming good missionaries from those who have gone before us. This is good and learning from them helps us be better servants. However, there has never been a missionary like you, and so it is critical that while you are in the Missionary Training Center, you develop the ability to reason with the Lord. If you can learn to access the Spirit of the Lord, He will enlighten your mind and your mission will be filled with relevance and purpose.

The ability to do this is important because there are many things that happen so unexpectedly; things that often perplex us. I have learned often through sad experience that when I get to a situation like this, where I am tempted to seek grand manifestations to address life's intervening circumstances, often called unintended consequences, or as Elder Maxwell calls them, "life's tutorials," when I do so, I certainly always come to grief. The response to these unintended consequences is the subject of Letter Four, so for now, seek His will as was shown in the Lord's Prayer, and we often find our will swallowed up in His and thus we are learning by the Spirit! Think deeply in terms of still, small but very meaningful events; ponder the truths you are learning and they will stay with you forever.

With warm personal regards,

LETTER FOUR

THE MTC AND THE SECOND IMPORTANT LESSON TO LEARN

If the ability to learn by the Spirit is the first valuable lesson, then the second important lesson is to understand the law of unintended consequences.

Dear Missionary:

In my last letter, we discussed a self-evident but important truth. The Holy Ghost is the most important gift you have in discerning truth. It is often a still and quiet gift that requires you to nourish it by tender and small means. We learned that by these small things are great things brought to pass, even miracles. We have learned that by these small steps, your testimony will become strong, like one built in bedrock. I know that as you entered the Missionary Training Center, you entered a time that may be of intense scrutiny and therefore it is one of those times when things can be difficult. To be placed in an environment where life is entirely different than the one you lived before is definitely an adjustment. I understand very well where you are. I know one of your many admirable goals to be achieved in serving a mission would be to help people come to Christ and find the joy that comes in building a solid relationship with the Lord and His church. In that regard, you must now realize that one can never know for sure how the Lord will use this experience found in the MTC to help you effectively reach this admirable goal, but He will use it. Therefore, you must trust in Him and Him alone.

I have found that we all have expectations of what the future will be like and as we come to embrace that future, people like you have a plan as to what you want to do and how you want to achieve it. Often, however, these plans change as circumstances change. We all need training by those who have trod this path before to help us avoid pitfalls often encountered by missionaries. This training makes us more effective servants as we try to maximize our time, whether it be for 18 or 24 months. This time frame, although it may seem to be a long time, is really very short. Each hour should be used effectively. In that regard, we are trained to be effective missionaries in ways that are unfamiliar to us. This is called social engineering and as we go forward in our service in the church, we will be trained to find more effective techniques so that we can exercise our office in ways that make us more successful while serving others. Such steps are undertaken so that we can make a plan, usually along the lines they have outlined, to be able to find that success.

This is good council, and it will help you become a more useful missionary in the service of the Lord, but such engineering must be tempered with the fact that events in life cannot be predicted with certainty. This means that at best, our planning and our expectations can only be of a provisional and exploratory nature. Life itself will intervene and circumstances **will** change. These changes are, in most cases, unexpected and unanticipated for both good and ill. This is what is happening to you now. You must give it a chance. I know that you try every day to make the experience there a great one. This is your nature and one of the things I most admire and respect about you. You think about things deeply and are motivated by great dreams of things that you can accomplish. I share enthusiasm for your abilities and you will, no doubt, be successful in the endeavors of life.

So, it is natural that when you are put into an environment where the means of accomplishing those goals in your mind diverges from the plan, such deviation creates a sense of frustration. So perhaps this too will be an experience in the way life can be and thus serve as a tutorial (as Elder Maxwell likes to call these kinds of experiences) in which patience, and other Godlike attributes can be developed. Max Weber, the father of the science of sociology, suggested that every action always creates "unintended consequences," which in and of themselves define life. You have come on a mission to achieve certain purposes. **It is the purpose of this letter to teach you the second most important lesson to be learned at the Missionary Training Center, how to deal with these - as Weber explained - unintended consequences of life.**

When I get to a situation like yours, experiencing life's intervening circumstances, unintended consequences, or, as Elder Maxwell calls them, life's tutorials, the first question I always ask is "What does the Lord want me to learn from this?" As I explained, when I make these circumstances part of my prayers and as I seek to be on His agenda by seeking His will, I really find my efforts at prayer to be very fruitful. The Lord seems to recognize my dilemma and the Spirit talks to me and helps me to see what lessons for my life the Lord intends from these. The second thing I do is pray for strength. I share your zeal never to quit and because I do, I have found if I don't pray for strength and answers, I become "bruised and bloodied" from my efforts without understanding. I become a victim of the "zeal without knowledge" syndrome. In this state, I need to trust the Lord, for now, since there is no one else in whom to trust.

By attempting to subordinate my will to to the Lord, I find that my spirit becomes more malleable and pliant. In that light, let's turn to the writings of Elder Neal A. Maxwell:

> When we really learn of the Savior, it will be by taking His yoke upon us. Though this is a severe form of learning, there is no other way. When thus yoked, we get much more learning than we bargained for. Nor is His yoke to be removed partway down life's furrow, even after a good showing up to the present. Those who are meek sense, at least in part, what is actually underway even in the midst of this [tutorial] schooling...Meekness helps us surmount the stumbling blocks so that we are prepared to receive a deeper and wider view. (*Meek and Lowly*, pages 1 and 76.)

As I think of possible answers the Lord may wish to share with you, my good friend, as your mission unfolds, I am overwhelmed with the number of possibilities that are open to you. I know that the MTC can seem at times a bit too structured, but when one takes the "deeper and wider view," one will realize that this is the most effective way to take a disparate group of young men and women and quickly mold them into effective missionaries especially given the fact that we only have 18-24 months for such an important work. You will find yourself at some point in your mission with either a difficult companion or hard work that feels unrewarding, and it will be at this time that you may think back on your MTC experience. You will then realize that it was a preparation for the things to come. The "deeper and wider view" of your current situation could then be expanded and generalized to your broader mission experience.

I love the Bible and I love the writings of Paul. We use the King James Version and it is truly the best. Here is why. It is because the word itself retains its power when the Holy Ghost is present in the words. When we look at a comparison between the original translators of the King James Version of the Bible and the account of its modern intellectual Revisers, we learn from such a comparison something that is very instructive. We learn from President J. Reuben Clark, the following:

> The original translators of the King James Version stated in 1611: Truly good Christian Reader, we never thought from the beginning that we should need to make a new translation, nor yet to make a bad one a good one; but to make a good one better, or out of many good ones, one principal good one, not justly to be excepted against; that hath been our endeavor, that our mark...And in what sort did these assemble? In the trust of their own knowledge, or their sharpness of wit, or deepness of judgment, as it were in an arm of flesh...They trusted in him that hath the key of David, opening, and no man shutting; they prayed to the Lord, the Father of our Lord, to the effect that St. Augustine did; O let the Scriptures be my pure delight; let me not be deceived in them, neither let me deceive by them. In this confidence, and with this devotion, did they assemble together. (*Why the King James Version,* page 419.)

With that in mind, however, I would like to quote to you a passage from the Book of Hebrews from the Revised English Bible. President Clark has told us why we use the King James version of the Bible, but because it seems to emphasize better the point I am making to you, I will use the Revised English translation. In Hebrews 12:7-11, it reads. *"You must endure it as discipline: God is treating you as sons. Can anyone be a son and not be disciplined by his father? If you escape the discipline in which all sons share, you must be illegitimate and not true sons. Again, we paid due respect to our human fathers who disciplined us; should we not submit even more readily to our scriptural Father, and so attain life? They disciplined us for a short time as they thought best; but He does so for our true welfare, so that we may share his holiness. Discipline, to be sure, is never pleasant; at the time it seems painful, but afterwards those who have been trained by it reap the harvest of a peaceful and upright life."*

Well, it seems in these verses that the "deeper and wider view" we are talking about is discipline and meekness (this is not weakness). Meekness allows us to put into perspective the unintended consequences of life and see with a "deeper and wider view." Meekness, that indispensable attribute to deal with unintended consequences, is developed, not surprisingly, through a broken heart and a contrite spirit. In order to be able to cope with the unintended consequences of life, which, as we have explained, define how life is to be lived, a great corollary that must be attached. It is this: **an important consideration to take into account when dealing with unintended consequences must be to always maintain a deeper and wider view of the current situation in which we find ourselves.** If this lesson is well learned, it will help us to develop meekness in response to unintended consequences. This in turn will help every missionary find the most success in the mission field itself. It is the discipline of the situation found at the Missionary Training Center that asks us to trust God, to ask Him what we should learn from this situation so that we may obtain the "deeper and wider view."

It is my experience in life, having gone through many trials (some of my own making and some not) that life is a time where the

Lord will discipline us so that we will become stronger and better able to deal with the intervening circumstances that invariably do come into our lives. We learn that we can trust the Lord and He will deliver us and teach us. If we are not meek, we cannot trust Him because we are too set on finding our own path. This becomes too willful, if I may be so bold to suggest, that in our zeal for success, we need perhaps to be more thoughtful and prayerful in seeking to plow around these obstacles instead of zealously trying to plow right through them. We would know what to do if we were meek and teachable and were able to cultivate that most important trait, to learn by the Spirit.

You are anxious to learn and are quick to follow the counsel of the Spirit. Try this out: ask the Lord what you are to learn from this experience and which of the many options that lay before you, should you choose? See if He does not answer your prayer, even as you reason with Him in the manner He prescribed and discussed in Letter Three, which concerned itself with learning by the Spirit. Put this experience into the perspective of developing greater meekness and discipline, which will also place the needed social engineering found at the MTC into its proper context. This learned behavior comes from those who study organizational behavior and through it we have found useful tools that help us be more effective and efficient. However, if we do not apply scriptural perspective to this approach we then turn the social engineering experience into one of corporatism where we view the teaching techniques mastered as salesmanship, or worse, marketing. These are business tools that are good within their methodological context as tools of presentation, but we must never forget that they are no substitute for understanding the doctrines of the restored gospel.

In fact, if we do not keep them in their proper context, they can indeed damage our testimony and create a blind spot for us. Why is this so? It is because if we are not careful, we depreciate the great and marvelous truths the restoration has brought to us. We ask facile questions, such as, "How does the gospel make me a more marketable commodity in the world of commerce?" Or worse, we ask, "Does any of this matter to my 'real' life?" When we teach the doctrines of the gospel, we will see that the doctrine is in fact our greatest strength. When presented with meekness, we tell every person who will listen to bring to us all the truth they have, and let us add wonderful things to that truth. In response to questions regarding secular application as opposed to doctrinal understanding, we ask, as Alma did after explaining the doctrine of faith, in Alma 32:35, *"O then, is not this real? I say unto you, Yea, because it is light; and whatsoever is light, is good, because it is discernible, therefore ye must know that it is good..."* So in fact, it is in the discipline of the Spirit which comes to us because of our meekness that our confidence in the Lord will grow; we find then that: *"...the Lord thy God shall lead thee by the hand, and give thee answers to thy prayers."* (Doctrine and Covenants 112:10.)

With warm personal regards,

LETTER FIVE

THE THIRD MOST VALUABLE LESSON – AVOIDING PRIDE

Pride is the universal sin. It is ever present in our lives but has a strange propensity to engulf us as we enter missionary service. This letter is fundamental on how to avoid it.

Dear Missionary:

What a thrill it was to get your letter! We discussed the first two principles you need to learn in Letters Three and Four. They are: first, to learn the correct way to perceive the Spirit of the Lord so you may be able to both learn and teach by that Spirit; second, the invaluable role of meekness and of bringing forth the sacrifice of a broken heart and a contrite spirit, as we respond to life's unintended consequences. We will now build on these two lessons to find **the third most valuable lesson to be learned: the ability to recognize and avoid pride.** Alexander Solzhenitsyn wrote, in his trilogy about the repressive Soviet prison system *(The Gulag Archipelago – 1918-1956, I and II)*, "Pride grows in the human heart like lard on a pig." It is part of the universal fallen condition of man and is omnipresent in our world.

A good number of missionaries who are in the MTC know very little about the gospel and thus find it easy to be caught up with this malady. With better preparation now being undertaken in the stakes, this situation should improve. I know you are prepared to be a missionary. You were very diligent in your studies before your mission and learned about pride, but we now need to go deeper. The fact that a number of missionaries come unprepared to the Missionary Training Center does account for the fact that the gospel presented there is very basic, and to you seems to be accomplished by the use of platitudes. Platitudes are simple or trite expressions that require little thought to understand; or are such broad expressions that almost any meaning can be attached to them. The Lord deals with these missionaries who are not prepared in this way, at the MTC, so that they may walk before they try to run.

For those who have prepared well, it sometimes becomes a small trial to hear platitudes every day for which there seems to be no thought. In cases like this, from Letter Three: remember to be meek and teachable. These spiritual platitudes are for the unlearned missionary who has come on his or her mission unprepared, but if you are meek, you will uncover unexpected truths even in platitudes. You must seek to be a true disciple as you help others less fortunate become committed and effective servants. Without the preparation and faith of the better prepared, many of these would never make it. It is truly a miracle that most all become prepared enough to begin to find success in the mission field itself but we all must build on that preliminary preparation.

After your exposure to life at the MTC, you now see why I feel so strongly about scripture study and missionary preparation. You get very little of it down there because of the needs to prepare the "self" with proselyting techniques and the need some have to learn a foreign language. However, this lack of exposure to the scriptures often leads to a shallow understanding of them, which if present, often leads missionaries to comprehend the scriptures in a platitudinal way. This means that such comprehension is trite and shallow which then leads to a doctrinal misunderstanding that could be quite detrimental to your testimony. Because you did prepare well, try to put your scriptural knowledge into the context of *Preach My Gospel*. There, the Spirit will lead you and just as you did during the preparation course, you will find enumerable "ah-hahs" that will feed your spirit. Your time at the MTC will become more productive as the new missionaries get better acquainted with the gospel. As these new missionaries feel the Spirit, which is there in rich abundance, this will happen and your joy will grow to a new level. The tragedy however, is that some never escape the level of platitude during their entire lives and hence never know the real joy of understanding the gospel.

As I read your letter, I was so impressed with its honesty and candor. That is one of your great strengths, my friend. Now, let's see if we can't approach these concerns you raised from a different vista and discover new truth, which will be of benefit to you. I want to start with missionaries who think that they know it all. I too, have problems with people like this and true, the stem of this problem is found in pride. This is a common problem in the world and unfortunately also in the church. It is omnipresent in all venues of life. Some priesthood leaders and some missionaries suffer from this malady and think their calls were special, written on the stones of Sinai by the finger of the Lord. When this is the case, they begin to treat all of us, whose calls they incorrectly perceive came in a less inspired way, as "inferiors." This experience leads us into the third most valuable lesson and shows us why we need to avoid pride.

Let's turn to the scriptures and see what the Lord has said concerning this condition. In Doctrine and Covenants, Section 121:34-40 we read, *"Behold, there are many called, but few are chosen. And why are they not chosen? Because their hearts are set so much upon the things of this world, and aspire to the honors of men, that they do not learn this one lesson – That the rights of the priesthood are inseparably connected with the powers of heaven, and that the powers of heaven cannot be controlled nor handled only upon the principles of righteousness. That they maybe conferred upon us, it is true; but when we undertake to cover our sins, or to gratify our pride, our vain ambition, or to exercise control or dominion or compulsion upon the souls of the children of men,* **in any degree of unrighteousness***, behold, the heavens withdraw themselves; the Spirit of the Lord is grieved; and when it is withdrawn, Amen to the* *priesthood or the authority of that man. Behold, ere he is aware, he is left unto himself, to kick against the pricks, to persecute the saints, and to fight against God. We have learned by sad experience that it is the nature and disposition of almost all men, as soon as they get a little authority, as they suppose, they will immediately* **begin to exercise unrighteous dominion***. Hence many are called but few are chosen."*

We see from the above, that it is the nature of all of us to exercise some form of unrighteous dominion over our fellow beings at some time in our lives. This describes the social Darwinism that prevails among people who live in a telestial world and believe me, it is true telestial behavior. This is the way it is in the world; a world in which meekness and a broken heart is despised, where the sin of pride and unrighteous dominion infects all levels of society. We see it in corporate America, in the legal profession, in science, in education, and even in the church. All of us manifest telestial behavior when we don't enjoy the Spirit.

The only way to get rid of this is to bring forth a broken heart and a contrite spirit, something we discussed at length in our preparation course and a subject I revisited in my first four letters to you. By seeking the broken heart, we become meek and develop a gentler disposition. We therefore do not want to compel our brothers and sisters to do anything. We are kind and gentle because the Spirit of the Lord is within us. We are without pride and possess a real love of God and our fellow beings. Unfortunately, when human relations become tense, we do not see this very often in most people. We expect our priesthood leaders to be full of the Spirit and when they are not, when they act in hypocrisy and condescension, we can become cynical and faithless. Cynicism is also a manifestation of pride.

We see both pride and cynicism when we look closely at the rivalries between universities. We see such pride manifest between Harvard and Yale, between BYU and the University of Utah, and between Michigan and Ohio State. This is a big problem between the rivalry schools and it promotes a real elitist attitude on the part of each school. Fortunately within the state of Utah, we have many fine institutions of higher learning and a student attending any of them can receive a fine education if that student puts forth the required effort. In reality, for comparison purposes between BYU and the U of U, the law schools at both universities are highly ranked; the BYU school of accounting is ranked in the top ten of comparable schools; the University of Utah College of Medicine, where Cecil Samuelson, the a past president of BYU, was once the dean, is top ranked as one of the world's best and it is globally much sought after. Both schools have contributed prodigiously to the leadership found in the church. A majority of members of the Quorum of the Twelve for the past 125 years attended the University of Utah. Brigham Young University has also produced some of our finest church leaders.

    The kind of talk we often hear among our schools comes from hubris and a sense of pride, which is an ugly trait no matter where it is found. In fact, in Utah, we are well-served by all of the following: Brigham Young University, the University of Utah, Utah State University, Weber State College as well as the University of Southern Utah, Dixie State University, Utah Valley University and even the Salt Lake Community College and the LDS Business College. Can you now see how blessed we are to have so many universities and colleges here? All should be respected and honored. The point is that such a debate is silly. If we are filled with meekness and love, if we have a broken heart and a contrite spirit we wish for the success of all good men and women everywhere. We want all to receive the truth and must resist the temptation to put anyone down. If we do not, we distance ourselves from the Spirit of the Lord and cannot completely feel His presence. I know this for myself due to my own weakness in this area. The Lord has regularly called me to repentance because I see a situation that is not correct, and then do not handle myself in harmony with correct principles. I am ever learning the things I now am telling you.

    Are there examples of really meek men in the scriptures? The answer is yes. We read in Numbers 12:3, "*Now the man Moses was very meek, above all the men which were upon the face of the earth."* In Psalms 25:9 we read, "*The meek will he guide in judgment: and the meek will he teach his way."* We know that the "meek shall inherit the earth", but we also have evidence, in a telestial or Darwinian sense, that the strong get many of the short-term rewards. We read further that the Savior was also meek, "*Take my yoke upon you, and learn of me; for I am meek and lowly in heart: and ye shall find rest unto your souls.*" (Matthew 11:29.) I guess that Moroni said it best (Moroni 7:42-44) when he said, "*Wherefore, if a man have faith he must needs have hope; for without faith there cannot be any hope. And again, behold I say unto you that he cannot have faith and hope, save he shall be meek, and lowly of heart. If so, his faith and hope is vain, for none is acceptable before God, save the meek and lowly in heart; and if a man be meek and lowly in heart, and confesses by the power of the Holy Ghost that Jesus is the Christ, he must needs have charity; for if he have not charity he is nothing; wherefore he must needs have charity.*"

Meekness to me means a lack of pride. We Latter-day Saints can become the most prideful people on earth; I never cease to marvel how quickly we seem to have answers to problems and run in, "like fools, where angels fear to tread!" President Ezra Taft Benson, in his classic talk on pride knew this and therefore gave us a corrective:

> Most of us think of pride as self-centeredness, conceit, boastfulness, arrogance, or haughtiness. All of these are elements of the sin, but the heart, or core, is still missing. The central feature of pride is enmity – enmity toward God and enmity toward our fellowmen. Enmity means "hatred toward, hostility to, or a state of opposition." It is the power by which Satan wishes to reign over us. Pride is essentially competitive in nature. We pit our will against God's. When we direct our pride toward God, it is in the spirit of "my will and not thine be done." As Paul said, they "*seek their own, not the things which are Jesus Christ's*" (Philippians 2:21). Our will in competition to God's will allows desires, appetites, and passions to go unbridled (see Alma 38:12; 3 Nephi 12:30). The proud cannot accept the authority of God giving direction to their lives. (see Helaman 12:6.)
>
> They pit their perceptions of truth against God's great knowledge, their abilities versus God's priesthood power, their accomplishments against His mighty works. Our enmity toward God takes on many labels,

such as rebellion, hard-heartendness, stiffneckedness, unrepentant, puffed up, easily offended, and sign seekers. The proud wish God to agree with them. They are not interested in changing their opinions to agree with God's. Another major portion of this very prevalent sin of pride is enmity toward our fellowmen. We are tempted daily to elevate ourselves above others and diminish them (see Helaman 6:17; Doctrine and Covenants 58:41). The proud make every man his adversary... (see *Ensign*, May, 1989.)

From this we see that the central feature of pride is enmity toward God and our fellowmen. It is our pride that causes us to feel we are better than the next man and it is our pride that causes us to feel offended by other's behavior. Sin is the only action that truly is offensive. Even then we should still love the sinner. If we see priesthood leaders who seem to feel they are better than the rest of us, President Benson's talk has direct application to them. As we noted, there are those within the Church that fall into this category, and you seem to have met some of them. However, when we react with a prideful attitude, we too, reject the Spirit. Hence, when you tell me that you don't feel the Spirit, and that you recognize that you are feeling prideful, I say you are making great progress. The last question concerning this subject becomes, "How does one deal with this issue within ourselves and with others?"

I think a good example to begin with is Ammon. In Alma 17:22-23, 25 we read, "*And the king inquired of Ammon if it were his desire to dwell in the land among the Lamanites, or among his people. And Ammon said unto him: Yea, I desire to dwell among this people for a time; yea, and perhaps until the day I die...But Ammon said unto him; Nay, but I will be thy servant...*" We see that Ammon wanted to preach the gospel to the Lamanites who were arrogant and proud. To gain their confidence, Ammon asked if he could be a servant and thus wait for the Lord to give him strength and deliver the Lamanites to him when they would be ready to hear the gospel. Ammon waited until the Lord delivered to him the victory, and what a victory it was. Lamoni and his entire household were converted because Ammon was meek. Isaiah

40:28-29 and 31 states, "*Hast thou not known? hast thou not heard, that the everlasting God, the LORD, the Creator of the ends of the earth, fainteth not, neither is weary? there is no searching of his understanding. He giveth power to the faint; and to them that have no might he increaseth strength...But they that **wait** upon the LORD shall renew their strength; they shall mount up with wings as eagles; they shall run, and not be weary; and they shall walk, and not faint."* We see that we must rely on the Lord to deliver the required results. If we are meek, we will see Him moving in His heavens and we will rely on Him to deliver us, and He will if we have faith and hope, because of our meekness.

With meekness, we develop a desire to assist the Lord in doing His great work. We found, as we studied and prepared for this great calling, that unless we were meek, our ability to assist Him would be diminished. We began our study early on by reading section 4 of the Doctrine and Covenants starting in verse 3: "*Therefore, if ye have desires to serve God ye are called to the work; For behold the field is white already to harvest; and lo, he that thrusteth in his sickle with his might, the same layeth up in store that he perisheth not, but bringeth salvation to his soul; And faith, hope, charity and love, with an eye single to the glory of God, qualify him for the work. Remember faith, virtue, knowledge, temperance, patience, brotherly kindness, godliness, charity, humility, diligence. Ask, and ye shall receive; knock, and it shall be opened unto you. Amen.*" Do you not see here, my dear friend, that nowhere in this verse does the Lord tell us that a certain number of our works is required? No, we are required to simply thrust in our "sickle," meaning have the desire to preach. With this said, we are qualified if we remember and cultivate the attributes given. If we rely on Him by asking Him and knocking on His door, He will open His tremendous stores of knowledge and strength to us. He will show us how to do His work and He doesn't require us to prepare a catalogue of deeds to qualify us for service. Our efforts are required to develop the attributes mentioned in these verses, and these attributes are those of a meek, justified man. For truly Lehi stated so correctly, "*Behold, he offereth himself a sacrifice for sin, to answer the ends of the law, unto **all those***

who have a broken heart and a contrite spirit; and unto none else can the ends of the law be answered." (see 2 Nephi 2:7.) There it is again, the broken heart and the contrite spirit and this time we learn that without them, for us, the ends of the law (of mercy) cannot be answered.

We see that the scriptures are very clear that we need to develop the ability to have a broken heart and a contrite spirit so that we can have the Spirit with us, which is the gift given to all those who possess these attributes. When these attributes are with us, and we feel the Spirit of the Lord in our lives, we know that we are acceptable before the Lord. Thus, the Holy Spirit of Promise is sealing our lives and we are hence justified before the Lord. Being justified by the Spirit does not mean being perfect. When we are justified, we know that we are on the right path that will lead to eternal life. We read in Doctrine and Covenants 20:30-31, *"And we know that justification through the grace of our Lord and Savior Jesus Christ is just and true; And we know also, that sanctification through the grace of our Lord and Savior Jesus Christ is just and true, to all those who love and serve God with all their mights, minds, and strength."* So, therefore, even though full sanctification lies before us, even though we are not completely born again, we have the promise because of the doctrine of justification that this will happen if we continue on the path. This doctrine of justification is defined in Doctrine and Covenants Section 132:7 which reads, "*And verily I say unto you, that the conditions of this law* [justification] *are these: All covenants, contracts, bonds, obligations, oaths, vows, performances, connections, associations, or expectations, that are not made and entered into and sealed by the Holy Spirit of promise...are of no efficacy, virtue or force in and after the resurrection from the dead; for all contracts that are not made unto this end have an end when men are dead."* We see then that to have the Spirit of the Holy Ghost in our lives is vital for without it any work we perform has an end when we are dead.

So, how does all of this apply to you when you leave for your field of labor? Well, if we look at an example I think the point will be clear. If we are successful in baptizing people in our field of labor, should we take the credit? No, we give the credit properly to the Lord. We say that the Spirit taught and converted the candidate and we were just the instruments. This is a true statement. Therefore, the converse must also be true. If we don't baptize and we are teaching and doing the best we can do to be a good instrument, then we must also leave the results of not baptizing up to the Lord as well. We rarely do this, however. We often blame ourselves for not "working" hard enough or not binding the Lord enough due to a lack of faith. We impart tremendous feelings of guilt to each other for our "failures." This is wrong. If the Lord gives the baptisms, and if we are bringing forth justified efforts, then it is the Lord who sees our efforts, blesses and seals them for our good and then He takes responsibility for the results. If we would be meek, less "success oriented" and call more mightily on His name, we would trust in Him more to soften the hearts of those we are to teach.

It is very important to note, however, that if we are keeping rules, and are being obedient and humble, we must continue so to do. We do not need to behave like the priests of Baal, who tried in vain to elicit a response from their God (1 Kings 18:26 and 28-29): *"And they took the bullock which was given them, and they dressed it, and called on the name of Baal from morning even until noon, saying, O Baal, hear us. But there was no voice, nor any that answered. And they leaped upon the altar which was made...And they cried aloud, and cut themselves after their manner with knives and lancets, till the blood gushed out upon them. And it came to pass, when midday was past, and they prophesied until the time of the offering of the evening sacrifice, that there was neither voice, nor any to answer, nor any that regarded."* These priests of Baal thought that if **they** did great works of obeisance to their god, that he would answer them. We learn here that first, Baal was not God and second, because he was not, the behavior of the priests of Baal was one of pride and self-aggrandizement. Surely, a broken heart or a contrite spirit does not motivate such behavior.

Elijah, on the other hand, after pouring water over the alter three times so that the trench around the alter was full of water, then he prayed (verse 37-38), *"Hear me, O LORD, hear me, that this people* may know that thou art the LORD God, and that thou hast **turned their heart back again**. *Then the fire of the LORD fell, and consumed the burnt sacrifice, and the wood, and the stones, and the dust, and licked up the water that was in the trench."* Elijah prevailed because **his heart** was broken and it was this attribute, not all the great prideful prayers and demonstrations to Baal that carried the day. When we feel that we should act in exaggerated ways, even in ways that normally are approved of the Lord, it is pride straight through. And when we are motivated by pride, God will not answer these kinds of prayers or reverence these kinds of protracted efforts to impress Him. He knows that such exaggerated efforts at obedience are designed not for God, but only to be seen of men (Matthew 6:1-5), whether we worship the true God or Baal, the behavior evidenced by Baal's priests is offensive to Him who made us.

Our job is to wait upon Him, and bring a greater portion of the Spirit into our lives through repentance and sacrifice. This is deeply personal as is our commitment to the gospel. If we feel the Spirit in great abundance in our lives, and we still have not achieved that which we think we should achieve, be they baptisms, or achieving personal spiritual goals, then we must realize that we still are doing what the Lord would have us do, and we must be patient. Remember, we must wait upon the Lord. This is a fundamental Christ-like attribute. Elder Joseph B. Wirthlin taught us:

> We will have REAL joy and happiness only as we learn patience. Too often, we are impatient with ourselves, our family members, and even with the Lord. We demand what we want right now, regardless of whether we deserve it, whether it would be good for us, or whether it is right. (*Ensign,* May 1987, page 30.)

If others try to exercise "unrighteous dominion" over us, by telling us to behave like the priests of Baal, by asking us to abuse our bodies by not sleeping, or by telling us to fast for days just to impress the Lord, they are wrong; this is not the Lord's way. Priesthood leaders are called to help us gain the **gifts** of the Spirit and the assurance of the Lord, not to organize us to the point that we look to our own works and efforts for success and not doing the Lord's work the Lord's way with meekness and faith. Work and effort are absolutely required and missionaries who are lazy will not have the Spirit with them. We must work, but to what end? It is clear that our efforts must be done so that the Spirit of the Lord justifies these efforts; otherwise, we will not succeed. In other words, we must perform these efforts in meekness and with a broken heart and a contrite spirit.

This brings me to an important point. It is a simple fact we cannot "earn" or compel blessings from God. Such an expression, "earning" blessings, misunderstands the fundamental relationship between God and man. One who loves another and wishes to enhance the other generally gives gifts; the giver doesn't make the receiver "earn" the gift and the gift is given as a token of the relationship between the giver and the receiver. All who receive gifts from God do so based on the relationship they have developed with Him. What gifts do we give our Savior? In Doctrine and Covenants 59:3 and 7-8 we read, *"Yea, blessed are they whose feet stand upon the land of Zion, who have obeyed my gospel; for they shall receive for their reward the good things of the earth, and it shall bring forth in its strength...Thou shalt thank the Lord thy God in all things. Thou shalt offer a sacrifice unto the Lord thy God in righteousness, even that of a* **broken heart and a contrite spirit**.*"* So, if we bring forth a sacrifice of a broken heart and a contrite spirit and offer it as a gift to our Lord, then the good things of the earth (whatever that means) shall be theirs. It is not in economic terms that the Lord makes that statement; it may be, but most likely refers to the quiet assurance of eternal life, God's greatest gift (see Romans 6:23).

The relationship between God and man is not defined as employer/employee, nor is it defined in corporate terms of CEO/management. The relationship is one of Father to child, a Father that seeks all good things for His child and knows perfectly what that child needs. How often did the Savior command us to be like little children? (see Mosiah 3:19.) I realize that occasionally some of the brethren have used the word "earn" with respect to blessings. Sometimes they say we must "qualify" for the blessings, which is better. What do they mean by this? They are telling us we must seek to understand the Lord because the concept of "reward" or "earning" or even "qualifying" for blessings, if understood in an economic sense, is flawed. The Lord told us what our reward for obedience would be in Isaiah 32:17, he tells us, *"And the work of righteousness shall be peace; and the effect of righteousness quietness and assurance for ever."* It is important not to mix our metaphors. We must not be like the priests of Baal who thought exaggerated effort would compel their god to act. Although we cannot compel the Lord because we are obedient, we can in a relational sense serve Him and His needs by understanding His work and seeking to bring it to pass. In that way, we await His pleasure and accept His judgment.

All things of God, whether desire, faith, repentance, knowledge, healing, speaking in tongues (learning a language, for example), are gifts of the Spirit and come from the Lord. The defining attribute of the receiver is one who has a broken heart and a contrite spirit. I told you this subject is huge and in order to develop a healthy relationship with Deity, a man or a woman must be possessed of it. Our Savior is the example; when He made His supreme sacrifice for us, it was done both spiritually and literally through a broken heart. Thus, even the gift to see how the Lord works comes from God. When Nicodemus approached the Savior and asked what he needed to have eternal life, the Lord replied (John 3:3-5), "*Verily, verily, I say unto thee, Except a man be born again, he cannot **see** the kingdom of God. Nicodemus saith unto him, How can a man be born when he is old? can he enter the second time into his mother's womb, and be born? Jesus answered, Verily, verily I say unto thee, Except a man be born of water and of the Spirit, he cannot **enter** the kingdom of God.*" The Lord was teaching Nicodemus as well as us, that the things of the Lord must be received by first obtaining the Spirit so that we can see as He does.

And on what terms is the gift given? Not surprisingly, on the terms of a broken heart and a contrite spirit as we have previously read, "*unto none else will the ends of the law be answered*" (see 2 Nephi 2:7). Without the Spirit, the things of God remain hidden from our view. Once we can see, then what are the works we should do to enter the kingdom of God? We must be born of the water (baptism) and of the Spirit (receive the gift of the Holy Ghost) as the beginning of entering into the kingdom. Then, by first seeing through the lens of a broken heart and a contrite spirit, and seeking with all our hearts to do the things that we are directed to do, we will indeed be justified and our efforts will be given on His behalf to further His work. This concept of seeing and then doing justified works was taught plainly by the Savior to His disciples.

In Matthew 13:10-13, the Lord taught, *"And the disciples came, and said unto him, Why speakest thou unto them in parables? He answered and said unto them, Because it is given unto you to know the mysteries of the kingdom of heaven, but to them it is not given. For whosoever hath, to him shall be given, and he shall have more abundance: but whosoever hath not, from him shall be taken away even that he hath. Therefore speak I to them in parables: because they seeing see not; and hearing they hear not, neither do they understand."* So, my dear friend, we must be diligent in seeking the Spirit, and the Spirit will show us all things that we must do (see 2 Nephi 32:5). So, when pride is evident in our brethren, we must not react to it in a negative way. In 2 Nephi 2:26 we read, "...*And because that they are redeemed from the fall they have become free forever, knowing good from evil; to **act for themselves and not to be acted upon**...*" This means we can become like the Savior, Ammon, Moses and others who possessed meekness; we can act in an abundance of the Spirit. With the justifying influence of the Holy Ghost in our lives, our prayers become stronger, our knowledge increases and we "see" as the Savior sees.

My friend, the Lord has given us some very fine counsel, which I feel is especially directed at me because I am prideful and at times lose the Spirit and hence my vision. To maintain the Spirit in one's life requires what the scriptures call, heed and diligence (see Alma 12:9). The Lord said to us in 2 Nephi 32:7-9 something about those men who exercise unrighteous dominion over their brethren or who think they are better because they have the truth. Verse 9 is the indictment of men like me because I do not always follow this counsel and thereby lose the Spirit. The Lord through Nephi states in verse 7, "*And now I, Nephi, cannot say more; the Spirit stoppeth mine utterance, and I am left to mourn because of the unbelief, and the wickedness, and the ignorance, and the stiffneckedness of men; for they will not search knowledge, nor understand great knowledge, when it is given unto them in plainness, even as plain as word can be."* What we have discussed, about how to gain the Spirit and the relevant doctrines appended thereto, is true. There will be some that will dispute these things and say that we need to "earn" our way to the Lord, but the scriptures clearly do not sustain such a view. Even when confronted with references, some Latter-day Saints do not believe the Lord's word. Thus they "will not search knowledge, nor understand great knowledge." We must be patient with them and pray for them and sustain them in the position to which they have been called, for the Lord will deal with them; and if they are willing, He will teach them in His due time.

Now I come to verse 9. It always pierces my heart. *"But behold, I say unto you that ye must pray always, and not faint; that ye must **not perform any thing unto the Lord save in the first place ye shall pray unto the Father in the name of Christ, that he will consecrate thy performance unto thee, that thy performance may be for the welfare of thy soul.**"* When I am feeling proud and arrogant, feeling that I know everything, I think of this verse. Nothing I do, if not consecrated (justified) unto the Lord will be for the welfare of my soul. We must wait upon the Lord, bringing forth a broken heart and a contrite spirit and prepare to receive the gifts of the Lord. If I am overcome with a sense of "earning" my way, I begin to be puffed up with pride as I try to put the Lord in my debt. This cannot be; He is never in our debt and we are always in His. As the Spirit comes into our lives, we will desire to learn more, to do more and we will pray that our performance will be justified and be for our welfare. If we don't do this, the Spirit is grieved and even though we do wonderful works, the Lord will profess, as He did in Matthew 11, "I never knew you."

What I have written to you is true. Ponder and pray upon these things and I know the Lord will give you the witness of their application in your life. The rebellious nature of pride, as it is countered by the doctrines of meekness and of justification, which leads to being born again are inseparably linked. As we come to see the context of these doctrines, our mission will become far less complicated and we will be overcome by His goodness. We will seek to do His will and find joy in being His servant, even a suffering servant. He will deliver the victory to you on His terms and timetable; and I know *He will deliver!*

With much love, I remain your brother in the gospel,

LETTER SIX

MISSIONARIES MUST UNDERSTAND THE DOCTRINE OF GRACE, AGENCY AND JUSTIFIED WORKS

The understanding of these three doctrines and how they relate to each other are essential if you are to be a good and productive missionary.

Dear Missionary,

I am glad you are now beginning to understand the doctrine of justification and being "born again" of the Spirit. It will help you overcome pride, an affliction that affects all of us. By understanding the three important lessons to be learned at the Missionary Training Center, discussed in the previous five letters to you, that of learning by the Spirit, seeking meekness through a broken heart and a contrite spirit so that you come to understand the role of unintended consequences, and understanding the nature of pride and its danger to your soul, you are now able to understand the correct relationship you enjoy with the Lord. That relationship is defined as one of a father to a child, not of a CEO to employee, nor is its nature to be understood through any other relationship we find here on earth. As we fully unpack the meaning of such a relationship, it will help us understand that it is the Savior's works that both save and exalt us, not our own works, although we acknowledge we will have works and righteous works at that. And when we perform these works we realize we are enabling that great gift offered to us through the Atonement of our Lord, to more fully heal and reorder our lives. We need to now understand why this is so, and armed with that understanding, seek further justification of our works.

    You are now ready to explore this doctrine more deeply along with two others that are intertwined with the doctrine of justification by the Spirit and the acceptance by the Lord of works approved by the Spirit. These are the doctrines of agency and grace. We can now see how these attributes relate to justified works, meaning the Lord sending us His Spirit of peace as He approves of what we are doing. The definition of justification, as indicated in Letter Five, comes from Doctrine and Covenants 132:7 wherein we learned that all "works" not sealed by the Holy Spirit of Promise, meaning the Holy Ghost, are null and void when men (and women) are dead. This means all of our ordinances, contracts, even associations that are not sealed, meaning approved, by the Holy Ghost have no effect on our life after death. This fact guarantees that only those who have a broken heart and a contrite spirit will be able to receive the gift of repentance and improve the probation also given through the grace of Jesus Christ to us, his fellow-servants and thereby receive the blessings of exaltation and eternal life.

    Why is this so? It is because we cannot earn our salvation and exaltation as previously discussed in Letter Five to you. Our works are inferior to His works and it is by His works that we **receive, not earn** salvation and exaltation. Further, by adding this condition to the concept of works, the Lord has ensured that **unrighteous** works, meaning works that are solely for the purpose of "earning" our own way in, are rejected. President Harold B. Lee explained this assurance that works must be approved by the Spirit and that the motive for doing works at all is pure and not for the purpose of earning our way into the celestial kingdom. Works must be performed, as you might imagine, with a broken heart and a contrite spirit to be acceptable to God, for *"unto none else can the ends of the law be answered."* (2 Nephi 2:7.) Concerning the concept of being justified by the Spirit and not by works, President Lee taught:

> I want to comment about this one statement: "by the Spirit ye are justified." Now, I've been struggling with that statement, and I have found a definition that seems to indicate to me what I'm sure the Lord intended to convey. The definition that I think is significant says: "Justify means to pronounce free from guilt or blame, or to absolve, then we begin to see something of the office of the Holy Ghost..."
>
> I shall inject here another phrase that is oft discussed...This phrase where the Lord directs that all of these things are to be eternal, is, and "must be sealed by the Holy Spirit of promise." Let me refer first to the 76th section of the Doctrine and Covenants. Speaking of those who are candidates for celestial glory, the Lord says, *"They are they who received the testimony of Jesus, and believed on his name and were baptized after the manner of his burial...That by keeping the commandments they might be washed and cleansed from all their sins and receive the Holy Spirit by the laying on of hands...And who overcome by **faith**, and are sealed by the Holy Spirit of promise...* (Doctrine and Covenants 76:51-53.) In other words, baptism is only efficacious...and applicable when it is sealed [approved of] by the Holy Spirit of promise. (*Stand ye in Holy Places,* pages 51-52.)

So, we must do more to acknowledge His hand in all things. We must accept the gift He has brought to pass and offered to us. This approval by the Holy Spirit of Promise causes our souls to be reordered and meekness to become more of a way of life. We seek justified works, also known as good works, so that we may better mold ourselves in His image. Alma taught us about this reordering in Alma 5:13-14. In these verses Alma spoke of his father and the great reordering he experienced, *"And behold, he preached the word unto your fathers, and a mighty change was also wrought in their hearts, and they humbled themselves and put their trust in the true and living God. And behold, they were faithful until the end; therefore they were saved. And now behold, I ask of you, my brethren of the church, have ye spiritually been born of God?"* Alma is specifically telling us that it is trust in the Lord and His works, not in our works that produce the best results. This isn't easy; the path is filled with obstacles that require of us a lifetime of diligence. However, by starting a mission, you have made an important beginning. In the missionary preparation course and in my previous five letters, we have really focused on the broken heart and the contrite spirit.

Why, you may ask? The reason is we acknowledge the role of the Savior's work on our behalf, but what gifts can we give Him? As mentioned in the prior five letters, in order to present any gifts to Him, we need to possess these two attributes, the broken heart and the contrite spirit, in order to gain access to His presence. These precious gifts are some of the most refined gifts we can give to our Savior. If we analogize these gifts, we might say that we can liken them to a precious coin. On one side of the coin is the principle of love and charity; on the other side, we understand the law of sacrifice to be fulfilled in bringing forth a broken heart and a contrite spirit (see Doctrine and Covenants 59:8). These two gifts, charity on the one side of the coin and the broken heart and the contrite spirit on the other, we have acknowledged the fundamental values upon which living a Christian life is based. Charity and a broken heart are elements of love, even the pure love of Christ, and it is upon love of God and love of our fellowman, according to our Savior (Matthew 22:40), *"hang all the law and the prophets."*

I know that you have begun to make changes in your life along these lines and the questions you asked in your last letter reflect those important changes. Your questions further reflect your thoughts and feelings because as a result of reading Letter Five, you now want to explore more deeply why the "earning" of blessings is not correct. You are beginning to see that there are personal spiritual requirements needed to successfully accomplish the work of the Lord and these requirements have little to do with earthly success. Bringing forth the sacrifice of a broken heart and a contrite spirit, which allows us to receive the gift of faith, naturally leads us to a discussion about grace as it relates to agency, which in turn helps us to understand more closely the doctrine of justification of our works. To begin this discussion, let us turn to President Ezra Taft Benson, who discoursed regularly on the relationship between grace, agency and justified works. These subjects are not new. As we have discussed in Letter Five on pride, early in this dispensation, in Doctrine and Covenants 20:30-31, the Lord warned the sanctified. These are core doctrines President Benson explained in this 1984 General Conference address:

> The Book of Mormon is to be 'a standard unto my people, which are of the house of Israel,' said the Lord. (2 Nephi 29:2). It is a standard we should heed and follow. In the twentieth section of the Doctrine and Covenants, the Lord devotes several verses to summarizing the vital truths, which the Book of Mormon teaches. (See verses 17-36.) It speaks of God, the creation of man, the Fall, the Atonement, the ascension of Christ into heaven, prophets, faith, repentance, baptism, the Holy Ghost, endurance, prayer, **justification and sanctification through grace,** and loving and serving God. We **must** know these essential truths. ("A New Witness for Christ," Conference Report, October 1984.)

So we must know these essential truths and the way they interrelate to each other so that we may know the essential doctrines. Part of these doctrines included in the category of essential are the doctrines of grace, agency, and justification through grace, which then leads to sanctification also through grace, a subject for another letter.

I know that often when we speak of grace, we invoke Nephi's words (2 Nephi 25:23), *"after all we can do."* While this is certainly true, what is the context? What does it mean and how does it relate to grace? These concepts of grace, agency and the justification of works are associated together and if they are to be understood, they must be taken as a group; otherwise they are all highly misunderstood. We will discuss these again in future letters, but for now, as a prelude to that future discussion, we will discuss the relationship between grace, agency and justified works. Grace is defined many ways. The one I like the best is found in the Bible Dictionary which states:

> The main idea of the word is divine means of help or strength, given through the bounteous mercy and love of Jesus Christ...It is likewise through the grace of the Lord

that individuals, through faith in the atonement of Jesus Christ and repentance of their sins receive strength and assistance to do good works that they otherwise would not be able to maintain if left to their own means.

So we will begin with the above definition and let this explanation guide us as we discuss the relationship between grace and agency. We see that grace is an enabling power that comes to us as a gift from the Lord; it is derived from the work the Lord did in performing the infinite and eternal Atonement. Grace is a gift from God, and part of that gift comes to us as a gift of agency. If we do not understand that agency comes to us as a gift through the grace of God, we then think erroneously that our works are being performed outside the gift of grace, this leads us to incorrectly conclude that when we produce works, they are on the same level as God's work, which is in a sense, heresy. We think our works operate independently from God's work on an equal basis with His works, hence the misunderstanding of the phrase, "after all we can do." This is where the concept of "earning" one's blessings comes from. Because the relationship of equalizing our works with His is not right, we mistakenly conclude we must "earn" our own way, which cannot be done. Now, let's put grace within the framework of the Atonement; grace is indeed a gift, it is a gift that comes because of the Atonement to empower us with the divine means to do justified works, works approved by the Lord.

With this now in mind, let us begin to discuss the relationship between grace, agency and works. In Letter Five, we discussed 2 Nephi 2 and so your question regarding free agency as it relates to grace is a natural outgrowth of developing a broken heart and a contrite spirit. Let me begin first with agency. When we call agency "free agency," it underscores exactly what I just discussed above. By calling it thus, we think therefore that we are free to choose anything we want to and that our works, if we choose righteously, are measured as to be valued exactly equal to those of the Lord. This is false. As you read the scriptures, take special note of 2 Nephi 2, which is one of the most important chapters of scripture we have. It forms the basis of our understanding of critical principles of doctrine, such as grace and agency, and upon which other doctrines such as justified works build. It is essential to avoid a misunderstanding of other doctrines as well.

From Letter Five, we emphasized 2 Nephi 2:7 concerning the broken heart and the contrite spirit which were discussed in depth and from which we learned that unto only those souls that possess these traits will the effects of the Atonement apply. We will return to these all important traits or works a little later on in this letter. However, as a point of departure to the understanding of the relationship between grace, justified works and agency, the broken heart and a contrite spirit are preliminary requirements that will help us understand these doctrines. We first dealt with pride and the need for meekness and then we found that these traits, when offered to the Lord, were the traits that prompted Him to give us faith; they also were the foundation of coming to grips with the necessity of seeking justification for our actions. The desired justification cannot happen, as verse 7 has indicated, if we do not possess a broken heart and a contrite spirit, "...*and unto none else can the ends of the law be answered.*" Now let's see why this is so. Look at verse 5 in the same chapter. In this verse we learn, "*And men are instructed sufficiently that they know good from evil. And the law is given unto men.* **And by the law is no flesh justified...**" This verse therefore correctly teaches us that the works of the law cannot justify us. Why is this so? Because we are justified by the Spirit, and not by works done only to conform to the law. This is one reason why motive is everything. If we seek justification through our works only, without faith and without a broken heart and a contrite spirit, we are by definition trying to "earn" our way in. This is not possible because without faith (which comes from a broken heart and a contrite spirit as a gift to us) and without the gift of grace which gives us power to do justified works, our works would be moot and meaningless.

Now let us move to the reason Lehi taught this. It was because of what he wrote next that we see why our works, if perceived to be equal with God's works, do not justify us. These next verses put our works and the Lord's works into the right perspective (2 Nephi 2:8-9): "*Wherefore, how great the importance to make these things known unto the inhabitants of the earth, that they may know that there is no flesh that can dwell in the presence of God, save it be through the merits, and the mercy, and grace of the Holy Messiah, who layeth down his life according to the flesh, and taketh it again by the power of the Spirit, that he may bring to pass the resurrection of the dead, being the first that should rise. Wherefore, he is the firstfruits unto God, inasmuch as he shall make intercession for all the children of men; and they that believe in him shall be saved."* We learn from these verses that it is upon the works of the Messiah that we must rely for salvation, not upon our own works. Sometimes we think we can "work our way" to heaven, because we think our works are on an equal basis with His works; but this scripture clearly shows that Christ's work is the work that produces salvation and exaltation and not our works. Both Paul and Moroni have told us (Hebrews 12:2 and Moroni 6:4), that it is Christ who is both *"the author and finisher of our faith."* It is His work and not our work that is THE work of Salvation and Exaltation. It is our role to accept His work!

Our works are designed to bring the Spirit into our lives so that we can be justified; it is the Spirit that justifies us before the Lord and our justified works become the vehicle through which we bring the Holy Ghost into our lives. It is the Holy Ghost that helps us (through the enabling power of grace) to conform our priorities and values in a consistent manner to those of our Savior. This is why motive is so important. With the right motive, the Spirit will reorder our priorities to reflect His presence in our lives. Elder D. Todd Christopherson explains this very simply:

> The gift of the Holy Ghost...is the messenger of **grace** by which the blood of Christ is applied to take away our sins and [justify] sanctify us. It is also the Holy Ghost, in His character as the Holy Spirit of Promise, that confirms the validity and efficacy of your covenants and seals God's promises upon you. ("The Power of Covenants," Conference Report, April 2009.)

Therefore, it is the Spirit that justifies us and when we partake of the sacrament worthily, we feel this acceptance. This act then puts us in the position to accept the gift of sanctification also offered by the Messiah through His work. Sanctification makes us pure and clean.

When we are justified, that does not mean we are perfect. What it does mean is that the Lord approves the life we are living and is encouraging us to move forward on that path. Then, sanctification comes through the blood of Christ (see Moses 6:59), which cleanses us from all sin, and serves as the promised fulfillment made possible by justification. We can discuss this Letter Seven and Eight. So if we stay the course approved by the justifying influence of the Spirit, the promise of sanctification will be fulfilled. Let me see if I can't explain this more closely. Let's turn to 1 Nephi 15. Here, in verses 8-11, Nephi teaches his brothers that commandment keeping prepares our souls to receive the Holy Ghost. *"And I said unto them: Have ye inquired of the Lord? And they said unto me: We have not; for the Lord maketh no such thing known unto us. Behold, I said unto them: How is that ye do not keep the commandments of the Lord? How is it that ye will perish, because of the hardness of your hearts? Do ye not remember the things which the Lord hath said? – If ye will not harden your hearts, and ask me in faith, believing that ye shall receive, with diligence in keeping my commandments, surely these things shall be made known unto you."*

As it is plainly shown above, if we keep the commandments, the Lord will soften our hearts and we will receive His Spirit often in the form of spiritual gifts. The reason we call spiritual gifts, "gifts," is because they too cannot be earned. They are received through the grace of the Lord Jesus Christ. Some of the gifts are partially enumerated in the above scripture, as Nephi suggests, they will be given the gift of faith and through faith they will understand the other things the Lord does speak. When we turn to the Bible, we find the following (1 Corinthians 12:1-13), *"Now concerning spiritual gifts, brethren, I would not have you ignorant...Now there are diversities of gifts, but the same Spirit. And there are differences of administrations, but the same Lord. And there are diversities of operations, but it is the same God which worketh all in all. But the manifestation of the Spirit is given to every man to profit withal. For to one is given by the Spirit the word of wisdom; to another the word of* *knowledge by the same Spirit; To another **faith** by the same Spirit; to another the gifts of healing by the same Spirit; To another the working of miracles; to another prophecy; to another discerning of spirits; to another divers kinds of tongues...But all these worketh that one and the selfsame Spirit, dividing to every man severally as he will. For as the body is one, and hath many members, and all the members of that one body, being many, are one body: so also is Christ. For by one Spirit are we all baptized into one body, whether we be Jews or Gentiles, whether we be bond or free; and all have been made to drink into one Spirit."*

I placed emphasis in the above passage on faith so we can clearly see that it is a gift of the Spirit. Repentance, while not called out by Paul, is also a gift of the Spirit, as we discussed in Letter Two on worthiness, and as we learned there, it comes to us as a matter of God's grace; the grace He extends to us so that our probationary time can be wisely used. Indeed, there are infinite gifts produced by the Spirit through the grace and love of our Savior. It is interesting to note that Paul reserves a fullness of these gifts of the Spirit to those who have been baptized. Why? It is because only the Spirit can then truly justify those who have entered into a covenant with the Lord. This is a primary reason you are in the mission field. You are there to offer baptism and the conferring of the Gift of the Holy Ghost to those in the mission field. You will teach them it is the only way they can enjoy a fullness of the spiritual gifts, the culmination of these gifts being Eternal Life, to which the doctrine of justification by the Spirit of their works will lead. Without baptism and confirmation, this is not possible. Thus, we must be a member of the church to enjoy the Gift of the Holy Ghost, and through this gift and this gift alone can we be justified.

A full discussion of the gifts of the Spirit is a subject for another time, but it serves our purpose here to see that commandment keeping, done with a broken heart and a contrite spirit, betrays the intent of our hearts and thereby activates the Gift of the Holy Ghost. When this happens, accessing the works of the Messiah is achieved and we know by His grace that we are on the right path. Hence, Lehi's plea to Jacob (2 Nephi 2:8) *"Wherefore, how great the importance to make these things known unto the inhabitants of the earth, that they may know that there is no flesh that can dwell in the presence of God, save* **it be through the merits, and mercy, and grace of the Holy Messiah...**" This is an important underpinning for our faith. Without understanding this doctrine, we fall into the trap of trying to work our way to heaven and begin to rely on our own works. This is a BIG problem with many members of the church. Christ is the "*author and finisher of our faith*" (Hebrews 12:2). We want to make the Savior the author, but not the finisher. We misunderstand our own works and think that they provide the finishing and thus are a causal part of salvation and exaltation. This is clearly not so. Christ's works are the works upon which we need to rely for salvation.

Moroni further emphasizes this when he taught (Moroni 6:2-4). "*Neither did they receive any unto baptism save they came forth with a broken heart and a contrite spirit, and witnessed unto the church that they truly repented of all their sins. And none were received unto baptism save they took upon them the name of Christ, having a determination to serve him to the end. And after they had been received unto baptism, and were wrought upon and cleansed by the power of the Holy Ghost, they were numbered among the people of the church of Christ; and their names were taken, that they might be remembered and nourished by the good word of God, to keep them in the right way, to keep them continually watchful unto prayer,* **relying alone** *upon the merits of Christ, who was the author and finisher of their faith.*" As we have discussed in Letter Four, we now possess, to quote Elder Maxwell again, a "deeper and wider view."

Thus, we have deepened and broadened our understanding of the scripture, (2 Nephi 2:6-7), "*Wherefore, redemption cometh in and through the Holy Messiah; for he is full of grace and truth. Behold, he offereth himself a sacrifice for sin, to answer the ends of the law, unto all those who have a broken heart and a contrite spirit; and* **unto none else can the ends of the law be answered.**" In the final analysis we see how Nephi himself is an example of how this works. Let's look at 2 Nephi 4:32. Here we find Nephi bearing his testimony concerning the fact that it is upon the Lord's works we must rely. He bears us this witness, *"May the gates of hell be shut up continually before me, because that my heart is broken and my spirit is contrite! O Lord, wilt thou not shut the gates of thy righteousness before me, that I may walk in the path of the low valley, that I may be strict in the plain road."* Here is a justified man telling us that he has sins and temptations and because of them he falls short of the mark, just like all of us. But, he knows it is to the Christ that he must look to finally triumph.

Nephi had previously told us in verse 17 that his works were not sufficient, *"Nevertheless, notwithstanding the great goodness of the Lord, in showing me his great and marvelous works, my exclaimeth: O wretched man that I am! Yea, my heart sorroweth because of my flesh; my soul grieveth because of mine iniquities."* He then further confirms his trust in the Lord in verse 20-21 and 34 *"...My God hath been my support; he hath led me through mine afflictions in the wilderness; and he hath preserved me upon the waters of the great deep. He hath filled me with his love, even unto the consuming of my flesh...O Lord, I have trusted in thee, and I will trust in thee forever. I will not put my trust in the arm of flesh; for I know that cursed is he that putteth his trust in the arm of flesh. Yea, cursed is he that putteth his trust in man or maketh flesh his arm."* Nephi knows, and by his words so illustrates, that commandment keeping brings the Spirit. He offers the Lord a broken heart and a contrite spirit so that his works will show his faithfulness to the Lord. He never thinks that his works will be sufficient to bring salvation, and further, he never thinks that he has "earned" his way into the presence of God. Nephi knows that eternal life, as in all spiritual things, is a gift of God, even the greatest gift (Doctrine and Covenants 14:7).

So to sum up the first part of this letter and to better explain why we can't "earn" our salvation or exaltation, we see that we must rely on Christ's works. For Christ's works are far **superior** to our works; He is the "author and finisher" of our faith. Our works are the vehicle, if we seek to justify them, which will bring us the Spirit. The kinds of works we need to "put on the altar," are those that have been accompanied by a broken heart and a contrite spirit. These two traits are primary requirements to receive the gift of faith. If our works are not performed with a broken heart and a contrite spirit, they are performed without faith, and as such, do not access the Spirit of the Lord. If this is the case, we fall into the "deed doer" trap, relying upon our own works to bring salvation.

Alma's experience illustrates this point very well. When in the awful moment of his spiritual awakening, he declared (Alma 36:17-21), *"And it came to pass that as I was thus racked with torment, while I was harrowed up by the memory of my many sins, behold, I remembered also to have heard my father prophesy unto the people concerning the coming of one Jesus Christ, a Son of God, to atone for the sins of the world. Now, as my mind caught hold upon this thought, I cried within my heart: O Jesus, thou Son of God, have mercy on me, who am in the gall of bitterness, and am encircled about by the everlasting chains of death. And now, behold, when I thought this, I could remember my pains no more; yea, I was harrowed up by the memory of my sins no more. And oh, what joy, and what marvelous light I did behold; yea, my soul was filled with joy as exceeding as was my pain!"*

There is no "cheap grace" here. Alma didn't just "accept Jesus as his personal Savior, no he tells us he could remember his sins no more because of the Atonement which was to be wrought on behalf of mankind and in that Atonement, his change and transformation was contemplated. It was because of Christ's work, not his work, that this was even possible. Alma needed to accept the gift through repentance and baptism, but by having a broken heart (as he clearly illustrated he did), he rejoiced that the way was prepared through these ordinances to receive the gift of the Atonement. This concept was clearly understood and clearly taught in the Old Testament. King David writes in Psalms 51:16-19, the following, "*For thou desirest not sacrifice; else I would give it: thou delightest not in burnt offering. The sacrifices of God are a broken spirit: a broken heart and a contrite heart, O God, thou wilt not despise. Do good in thy good pleasure unto Zion: build thou the walls of Jerusalem.* **Then** *shalt thou be pleased with the sacrifices of righteousness, with burnt offering and whole burnt offering: then shall they offer bullocks upon thine alter."* Thus we see that our works are only justified when we have a broken heart and a contrite spirit. This has always been true throughout human history; even from the days of Adam, where he learned this truth from the very beginning of our probationary times. So too, even today, our works are not acceptable (justified) unless we perform them with a broken heart and a contrite spirit.

Let us conclude this part of the letter contrasting the view of man's works with God's works. The following two poems shall serve as an unswerving guide illustrating the nature of our works versus God's works. The first poem, entitled "Invictus" by William Ernest Henley shows how we sometimes arrogantly wish to put our works on an equal footing with His works; this illustrates the false understanding of "after all we can do." The second poem is Elder Orson F. Whitney's response to "Invictus". He was then a member of the Council of the Twelve and he clearly understood that our works are not remotely equal to the works the Lord has done for us and why relying on our works and not His works is folly:

INVICTUS

Out of the night that covers me,
Black as the pit from pole to pole,
I thank whatever gods may be
For my unconquerable soul.

In the fell clutch of circumstance
I have not winced nor cried aloud.
Under the bludgeonings of chance
My head is bloody, but unbowed.

Beyond this place of wrath and tears
Looms but the Horror of the shade,
And yet the menace of the years
Finds and shall find me unafraid.

It matters not how strait the gate,
How charged with punishments the scroll,
I am the master of my fate:
I am the captain of my soul.

ELDER WHITNEY'S RESPONSE:

Art thou in truth? Then, what of him
Who bought thee with his blood?
Who plunged into devouring seas
And snatched thee from the flood?

Who bore for all our fallen race
What none but him could bear
The God who died that man might live,
And endless glory share?

Of what avail thy vaunted strength
Apart from his vast might?
Pray that his Light may pierce the gloom
That thou mayest see aright.

Men are as bubbles on the wave,
As leaves upon the tree
Thou, captain of thy soul, forsooth!
Who gave that place to thee?

Free will is thine - free agency,
To wield for right or wrong;
But thou must answer unto him
To whom all souls belong.

Bend to the dust that head "unbowed"
Small part of Life's great whole!
And see in him, and him alone,
The Captain of thy soul!

With that in mind, let's now move on to the second part of this most important chapter, 2 Nephi 2. This deals with the gift of agency, another enabling power that comes because of the grace of the Lord and which is mentioned in Elder Whitney's poetic response. As I said in Letter Two, free agency is really moral agency and the following verses link grace and agency together. It is important that we understand the example that Lehi uses, for it illustrates how agency operates. He begins by stating that because of the Atonement, the "intercession" of the Savior, agency, like grace, exists in nature. Without the Atonement, there would not be grace or agency; there would be immediate consequences to our actions and therefore we would not be free to choose because there would not be any grace granted for incorrect choices. There would not be any agency either because without the grace accorded us by the Savior, we would lose the ability to choose life or death. One wrong choice would terminate our probation and there would be no time to repent.

Thus, as a consequence of the Atonement, there is opposition in all things and choice is made available to us; the consequences of making a wrong choice are held in abeyance until the time of probation is over. Lehi tells us in verse 11 (still in 2 Nephi 2) that if there was not opposition in all things, righteousness could not be brought to pass; likewise, wickedness also would not be present because we would not have any choice. Lehi tells us without the agency of man, there would be no progression; in verses 13-14, "...*all things must have vanished away...all things, both in the heavens and the earth...both things to act and to be acted upon.*" Hence, agency is an essential element for us and without it, we could not become like the Father

Now, to illustrate how agency operates, Lehi goes back to the beginning and to the creation of our first parents. This is the classic example of the cause and effect of agency, and is usually misunderstood by us unless we study and pray about it. We have already established that because of the Atonement, choice exists as a fact in nature. In verse 16, Lehi explains, "*Wherefore, the Lord God gave unto man that he should act for himself. Wherefore, man could not act for himself save it should be that he was enticed by the one or the other.*" In verse 17 we read further that Lucifer did choose one rather than the other in our pre-mortal life: "*And I, Lehi, according to the things which I have read, must needs suppose that an angel of God, according to that which is written, had fallen from heaven; wherefore, he became a devil, having sought that which was evil before God.*" Hence we see that agency was available to us in the pre-mortal life before we came here. Lucifer was able to choose evil while yet in the presence of God, which lets us know that even in the presence of the Lord, choice is possible. Because of the Atonement, choice is always possible, even in the millennium.

We know, therefore, through Lehi's teachings in 2 Nephi 2 that Lucifer became the administrator of evil in our world by using his agency to rebel against God in the pre-mortal life. We also had this agency in the presence of God in the pre-mortal life; we had the power to choose evil or good. The powers of evil are always present and preceded Lucifer becoming the devil. God did not create good or evil, they have always existed and even if Lucifer did not become Satan, it is my opinion that good and evil, just like matter and energy, have always existed independent of God. Choice and agency are parts and attributes of Godhood and exist with Him. If they are not present, He is not God, in fact cannot be God. This allows everyone the right to choose differently, even in His presence, although the consequences of our choices cannot be set aside except under the terms of grace, the first gift of the Atonement. We are now brought to the beginning of the earth experience and the creation of Adam and Eve. We see that they were created in a terrestrial state and were innocent. They had no knowledge of good or evil. They lived by the words the Lord gave them.

To understand how the Lord set all this up, we need to go to the Pearl of Great Price, specifically, Moses 3. Here we see the story of the creation told again as it was in the Old Testament. The Lord created the earth, all the plants, the animals and finally man. The Lord then gave Adam the following commandment in verses 16 and 17: "*And I, the Lord God, commanded the man, saying: Of every tree of the garden thou mayest freely eat, But of the tree of the knowledge of good and evil, thou shalt not eat of it, nevertheless,* **thou mayest choose for thyself, for it is given unto thee; but, remember that I forbid it, for in the day thou eatest thereof thou shalt surely die.**" Adam and Eve were given the parameters of their choices as well as the consequences of those choices.

We see here that the Lord gave Adam his choice, but told him the consequences of that choice. He forbade Adam the fruit because if he did not, there would be no choice, and undoubtedly Adam would have eaten the fruit as with all other fruits, and done so in innocence. Had this occurred, death would have naturally ensued from this act, not a choice, and the Lord would not be able to hold Adam accountable for this act because it would not have been a choice, just an event. Therefore, he was told he could eat of all other fruit without consequence, but when he partook of the fruit of the tree of knowledge of good and evil, the consequences had to have been explained to him. Why? It is because the partaking of the fruit of the tree of good and evil needed to be a choice. Had the consequences not been explained to Adam, and partaking of this fruit happened as a random act, then God would have been made a liar, having told Adam and Eve they could eat freely of every tree in the Garden. However, God is not a liar and tells us directly and straight up about the implication our actions have for both good and evil. The scriptures are full of His words that clearly and forthrightly tell us about the consequences of our actions.

If God had tried to trick us or not tell us completely about how significant the results of our actions were, He would, by implication in 2 Nephi 2, cease to be God. Because the Lord told Adam he had a choice, and the Lord told him the consequences of that choice, which were, if he ate of the fruit, he would die, preserved perfectly the principle of agency and confirmed the Lord's desire to be straight with Adam. Therefore, the pattern is set. He will likewise be straight with us, **you can rely on Him perfectly.** So, Adam and Eve were created and dwelt in the Garden of Eden in innocence. How long did they live in such a state? This was probably the case for a long period of time; how long, we don't know. As part of his creation, Adam had received other commandments, which because he was innocent, he could not follow. For example (Moses 2:28), "*And I, God, blessed them, and said unto them: Be fruitful, and multiply, and replenish the earth, and subdue it, and have dominion...over every living thing that moveth upon the earth.*" How were Adam and Eve to follow this commandment? Since they were created in innocence (see Moses 3:21-25), they did not have the requisite knowledge to follow this commandment, even though they were mature adults and sealed together as husband and wife by the Father Himself.

So we see that a perfect plan was put into place where Adam and Eve needed to gain additional knowledge, and the only way to gain that knowledge was to partake of the tree of knowledge of good and evil and have their eyes opened. The consequences of that action had been made known to Adam and Eve and hence the dilemma. The Lord had brilliantly preserved the right of agency by placing them in a situation where both Adam and Eve would need to make a choice. It was just as it was in the pre-mortal life. The commandments were not in conflict. A choice was given to Adam and to Eve through the grace of God; they needed to counsel together and make this choice. They could partake of the fruit, fall, gain knowledge and receive the gospel, which would bring them back to God in an exalted state, or without consequence, they could live as they had been created, in an innocent terrestrial state. The choice was theirs and theirs alone to make. The Lord did not force them to make it and in fact, could not force them to make it without ceasing to be God (see Alma 42:22).

What did Adam choose? Well in 2 Nephi 2:24-28, "*But behold, all things have been done in the wisdom of him who knoweth all things. Adam fell that man might be; and men are, that they might have joy. And the Messiah cometh in the fullness of time, that he may redeem the children of men from the fall. And because that they are redeemed from the fall they have become free forever, knowing good from evil; to act for themselves and not to be acted upon, save it be by the punishment of the law at the great and last day, according to the commandments which God hath given. Wherefore, men are free according to the flesh;* [and this due to Adam's choice] *and all things are given them which are expedient unto man. And they are free to choose* [because of the grace of God] *liberty and eternal life, through the great Mediator of all men, or to choose captivity and death, according to the captivity and power of the devil; for he seeketh that all men might be miserable like unto himself. And now, my sons, I would that ye should look to the great Mediator, and hearken unto his great commandments; and be faithful unto his words, and choose eternal life, according to the will of his Holy Spirit.*" The will of the Spirit is to seek justification of our works after bringing forth the requisite broken heart and contrite spirit.

We have one last item to consider. What is the role of Lucifer in all of this? His role **did not** affect the outcome of the plan in any way. The Lord had arranged the garden experience to produce a circumstance in which Adam was to choose. He did have enough knowledge to know he must choose but needed to gain additional instructions from the Lord. What the Lord had hoped for was that Adam and Eve would have put the whole problem before Him and He would have given them the further knowledge they needed to be obedient to all of the commandments they had already received. The Lord was confident that Adam and Eve would have chosen to pass through the experience we know as mortality because they had chosen to do so in the pre-mortal life. The moment at which Lucifer entered the Garden of Eden was not coincidental. Satan chose this moment, as he observed Adam and Eve, because it was at the time of innocence that he felt he could take best advantage of their newly discovered mortality.

From the beginning Lucifer has wanted to dethrone God. We read in Moses 4:1-4, "*And I, the Lord God, spake unto Moses, saying: That Satan, whom thou hast commanded in the name of mine Only Begotten, is the same which was from the beginning, and he came before me, saying – Behold, here am I, send me, I will be thy son, and I will redeem all mankind, that one soul shall not be lost, and surely I will do it; wherefore give me thine honor. But behold, my Beloved Son which was my Beloved and Chosen from the beginning, said unto me – Father, thy will be done, and the glory be thine forever* [talk about a broken heart and a contrite spirit!]. *Wherefore, because that Satan rebelled against me, and sought to destroy the agency of man, which I, the Lord God, had given him, and also, that I should give unto him mine own power; by the power of mine Only Begotten, I caused that he should be cast down; and he became Satan, yea, even the devil, the father of all lies, to deceive and to blind men, and to lead them captive at his will, even as many as would not hearken unto my voice.*"

We see therefore that Lucifer entered the Garden to see if he could once prevail there, as he had not in the pre-mortal life. The situation is exactly the same, only the venue is different. Satan came to Eve, and because he is the father of lies, he did not tell her the complete story. This is the way he **always** operates. He cannot tell the truth. He never tells the truth to anyone and hence there is so much confusion and falsehood in the earth. Consider the following (Moses 4:6): "*And Satan put it into the heart of the serpent, (for he had drawn many away after him,) and he sought also to beguile Eve, for he knew not the mind of God, wherefore he sought to destroy the world.*" The "many" referred to in the parenthesis are those that followed Lucifer in our pre-mortal life. You see, Lucifer sought to destroy the agency of man as we read above because if man has agency, he can thwart the power of Satan. Thus it was that Lucifer approached Eve; his motive being to destroy man's agency, by having him believe a lie. He thus thought he could thwart the plan accepted in the pre-mortal life by tempting Eve to partake of the fruit. We are informed from the above scripture that Lucifer does not know the mind of God and hence could not foil the plan that was adopted in our pre-mortal life.

How did Lucifer seek to destroy man's agency? Again we return to 2 Nephi 2. In verse 18 we read "*...Wherefore, he said unto Eve, yea, even that old serpent, who is the devil, who is the father of all lies, wherefore he said: Partake of the forbidden fruit, and ye shall not die, but ye shall be as God, knowing good and evil.*" By telling this lie to Eve, and if she ultimately would have believed it, Lucifer would gain power over the agency of man; he could thereby indeed be worshipped by Adam and Eve and their posterity. This is because they would have believed that simply knowing good from evil would empower mankind to become "gods" without the intercession of the Savior. This line of reasoning is exactly what he had used in our life before we came to earth. He told us all not to believe the Lord and one-third of the hosts of heaven did not believe the Lord and followed Lucifer (the many referred to above).

When Adam and Eve partook of the fruit, Lucifer thought the plan had been thwarted; not because they had eaten of the fruit, that was in the Lord's plan all along (as noted above), but because they had been obedient to him (Lucifer) and not followed God. He further thought that the spirits that followed him would now enter the bodies that Adam and Eve could now definitely create. It is also clear because of this that Lucifer did not know the mind of God. Perhaps Lucifer thought that once Adam had partaken of the fruit of the tree of good and evil that he would immediately partake of the tree of life as well. If that had happened, the plan of salvation would have been compromised as well. In Alma 42:5 we read, *"For behold, if Adam had put forth his hand immediately, and partaken of the tree of life, he would have lived forever, according to the word of God, having no space for repentance; yea, and also the word of God would have been void, and the great plan of salvation would have been frustrated."*

Because the Lord had provided a Messiah for us in the event of the decision to partake of the fruit, and if we accept the work of Christ, as Adam and Eve surely did, the effects of disobedience could be ameliorated through the Atonement. We thus come full circle. The Lord, through His grace, did allow a space for repentance. Likewise then, it is upon the works of Christ we must rely; His sacrifice and His Atonement open the way for all mankind to overcome the fall of Adam as a free gift. His works are clearly superior to ours because He is God and we are not. If we accept His gift and His grace, by making the appropriate covenants with Him, then our possibilities are endless. The Atonement thus preserves for us the choice of freedom and life as well as a choice for captivity and death. The inescapable conclusion is that without Christ, the agency of man is destroyed and without His grace, no probation could be granted. Therefore, all of our works, done without the justification of the Spirit, meaning works of "deed-doers," are inferior to His works. In every case however, our works are not enough to produce salvation. Since the Atonement is true and valid, the effects of sin and disobedience have been overcome subject to the conditions set down by the Savior to receive His gift. There is no such thing as "cheap grace" either. Grace enables us to be saved from our sins, not in them (see Alma 11:37).

Well my dear young friend, I have gone on way too long, but I hope this letter defines for you the concept of grace as well as the relationship between grace, agency and works. They are interrelated and an understanding of each of these doctrines is necessary to understand all of them. Agency, for example was granted to us as a grace from God. Our works, if not justified by the Holy Spirit of Promise, are not consecrated to us as a product of our faith, but become a source of pride and arrogance because we have discounted the works of the Lord in allowing us to bring forth these works. You have always been a good student and have a deep desire to be able to teach the truth. Continue to discuss these doctrines and foster the knowledge you are learning which will deepen your testimony. I will continually look forward to answering your new questions as you further grow in the gospel of Christ.

With much love and the warmest regards,

LETTER SEVEN

AS MISSIONARIES, WHAT ARE WE TO DO AND WHAT IS THE LORD TO DO

This subject is vital; we must come to know what we are expected to do and what we can expect the Lord to do. Much misery has come about when we try to force God to do things according to our will.

Dear Missionary,

The Missionary Training Center is really an interesting place. You have learned to maneuver well through the minefield of platitudes and those who exhibit "fake" spirituality; some missionaries use eloquent words but there is frequently no substance behind what they say. Generally, such a missionary's use of the word "should" is too much. This word is designed to produce a feeling of guilt in those to whom it is directed. There are people in authority that can use this word and use it properly to inspire our better behavior; but when random missionaries use this word, it often has a negative effect on us, as guilt, without godly sorrow, is not helpful. Why, you may ask? It is because guilt without godly sorrow paralyzes us, fills us with feelings of self-loathing and never inspires us to change. Now you know why I don't like the "should" word because it engenders this kind of behavior. The Spirit can't work with people completely and effectively until this kind of behavior, which is prideful, is overcome. This is common behavior for those who have yet to come to know the Master.

As a follow-up to Letter Six, concerning grace, agency and justified works, your next questions are both logical and show that you have thought about the relationship in great detail. You asked me an interesting question that deals with what we are to do and what we should leave to the Lord to do. You mentioned that some teachers in the Missionary Training Center teach that your place in the Kingdom of God is all up to you as if nothing is left to the Lord, and you properly ask, what does that mean? Let's lay a little ground work first before we answer this question directly. We have already discussed the fact that we can't "earn" our blessings. This is impossible because of the nature of our works versus God's work. They are not equal in any way. So, we must be careful not to confuse our works with His works and never assume our works are ever on the same level as His works. It is true that the Lord often uses us to accomplish His work, but if we confuse His works with our works, we become puffed up and prideful as noted earlier.

Having said that, we must also observe that the Lord has also told us that in fact, our works will judge us. We read in many places that this is true. Some examples now follow beginning in the Bible, in Romans 2:12-13 Paul taught us, *"For as many as have sinned without law shall also perish without law: and as many as have sinned in the law shall be judged by the law; (For not the hearers of the law are just before God, but the doers of the law shall be justified."* Further, in 1 Peter 1:17 we read, *"And if ye call on the Father, who without respect of persons judgeth according to every man's work..."* And finally in James 2:14 we read, *"What doth it profit, my brethren, though a man say he hath faith, and have not works? can faith save him?"* And then in verses 21 and 22 we further read, *"Was not Abraham our father justified by works, when he had offered Isaac his son upon the altar? Seest thou how faith wrought with his works, and by works was faith made perfect?"* In the Book of Mormon, in Alma 11:41, *"...for behold, the day cometh that all shall rise from the dead and stand before God, to be judged according to their works."* And again in Alma 41:3, *"And it is requisite with the justice of God that men should be judged according to their works; and if their works were good in this life, and the desires of their hearts were good, that they should also, at the last day, be restored unto that which is good."* So then, works are important, **not to earn salvation and exaltation,** but to demonstrate our willingness to **accept** the Lord's gift of His redemptive work; it is through **our works that we demonstrate our eagerness to receive His immeasurable gift to us of salvation and exaltation.**

Therefore, now that we understand the purpose of works, we ask, "Are some works of more value than other works?" The answer is, yes. There is a hierarchy among works of which we must be aware. The works that allow us to accept His gift are simple but profound. We must repent of our sins in the probation He has granted us through His grace and be baptized, so that we can receive the gift of the Holy Ghost. These are essential to salvation and essential for us to begin to make covenants with the Lord, and through these covenants, the promises of God to us are made sure. In Revelation 20:12-13, we read, *"And I saw the dead, small and great, stand before God; and the books were opened: and another book was opened, which is the book of life: and the dead were judged out of those things which were written in the books, according to their works. And the sea gave up the dead which were in it; and death and hell delivered up the dead which were in them: and they were judged every man according to their works."* What are these works, to be found in the book of life? What if these works are not found there?

We have demonstrated that without the gift of the Holy Ghost, there is no justification and no sanctification. There is no sealing by the Holy Spirit of promise, which allows the works we do to have eternal consequences. Consequently, the works to be found in the book of life referenced in the above scripture are those that have been sealed by the Holy Spirit of promise, giving such works eternal continuance. We already know that the works found there were not put in the book of life to demonstrate we have "earned" such a life, but they are there because the gift of the Holy Ghost has sealed them. What are the consequences of such a sealing? The effects of having works sealed by the Holy Spirit of promise are these: they have caused a great reordering of our soul and are those given that show we are being changed and made pure as we embrace this great gift. Bearing this in mind, there is a hierarchy of works that brings this change to pass. What is that hierarchy? First and foremost we must realize that these are the covenants by which the gift of eternal life is delivered to us. These works are contained in the First Principles and Ordinances of the Gospel: faith, repentance, baptism by immersion and the gift of the Holy Ghost (see Acts 2:38), and the ordinances performed in the temples of God. The Prophet Joseph Smith taught in Doctrine and Covenants 128:5, *"You may think this order of things to be very particular; but let me tell you that it is only to answer the will of God, by conforming to the ordinance and preparation that the Lord ordained and prepared before the foundation of the world, for the salvation of the dead* [and of the living]*..."*

There are other works, even works of merit that descend from these, and are cataloged as either celestial, those that are also sealed by the Holy Spirit of promise, terrestrial works that are not so sealed but are nonetheless extremely important and then there are telestial works which are good but pertain only to the affairs of this world. We see a further delineation of this hierarchy in Doctrine and Covenants 88:27-32, *"For notwithstanding they die, they also shall rise again, a spiritual body. They who are of a celestial spirit shall receive the same body which was a natural body; even ye shall receive your bodies, and your glory shall be that glory by which your bodies are quickened. Ye who are quickened by a portion of the celestial glory shall then receive of the same, even a fulness. And they who are quickened by a portion of the terrestrial glory shall then receive of the same, even a fulness. And also they who are quickened by a portion of the telestial glory shall then receive of the same, even a fulness. And they who remain shall also be quickened; nevertheless, they shall return again to their own place, to enjoy that which they are willing to receive, because they were not willing to enjoy that which they might have received."* Therefore we want to be sure that our works are celestial in nature. Note that the above verses point to "receiving" the gifts of the Lord, not "earning" them.

These verses further illustrate the different kinds of works and also highlight the works in which we are interested are celestial works. What can we conclude from the above verses? Well, first of all, we can conclude from the Doctrine and Covenants verses that there is a hierarchy among the works from which we can choose and so we should be discriminating and seek out celestial works. Second, from the verses in the Bible and the Book of Mormon we see that we indeed will be judged by our works, but we can also see that there can be a certain dialectic or tension between faith and works. This can be confusing. Some Protestants and Catholics, as well as many in our church, believe that we must "work our way to heaven." This again is an attempt to "earn" our salvation and we know that this is false, even from the Doctrine and Covenants, section 88 verses quoted above. Further, other Protestants believe in "cheap grace" in that we are saved by grace without the works of the law as Paul taught in Romans 3:26-28 when he stated, *"To declare, I say, at this time his righteousness: that he might be just, and the justifier of him which believeth in Jesus. Where is boasting then? It is excluded. By what law? of works? Nay: but by the law of faith. Therefore we conclude that a man is justified by faith without the deeds of the law."* This appears to be confusing and contradictory.

The apparent contradiction is resolved however, if we accept both premises as true, which we must, and in that we are saved by faith without the works of the law because it is the Savior's work that does the saving. However, in order to accept this great and final gift, we must do celestial works that allows the Spirit to justify such works, which then demonstrate to the Lord the kingdom after which we seek. So, then the contradiction is resolved when we come to understand and differentiate between our works and His works; since it is clear that we must have works. But it is also clear that we must have faith to accept His work as the true work of salvation and exaltation.

Let's elaborate on the above. Our first question then, is this: "What kind of works are included in the above scripture and what works are excluded by the Apostle Paul?" In other words, what is the difference between His works and our works and what must we learn about works so that we can differentiate between our works and His works? This question is vital, because if we fail to learn the difference, pride will become part of the equation, and we will try to earn our way back to God's presence with terrestrial and telestial works. We will incorrectly view every work we do, even if done arrogantly, meaning without faith, as a work that produces salvation and exaltation. This is of course false. The ability to see the difference among works and to differentiate between His work and our work **is absolutely vital to understand,** because if we don't understand the difference, we will find ourselves in a place where our worship becomes detached from the Spirit and without meaning. We then become distant from our Savior and from His healing waters. Further, in the worlds to come, we will be sorely disappointed.

Why will our misunderstanding of works produce such a poor result? The Savior Himself gave the answer when He placed works into their proper context. He told His disciples in Matthew 7:21-23, *"Not every one that saith unto me, Lord, Lord, shall enter into the kingdom of heaven; but he that doeth the will of my Father which is in heaven. Many will say to me in that day, Lord, Lord, have we not prophesied in thy name? and in thy name have cast out devils? and in thy name done **many wonderful works?** And then I will profess unto them, I never knew you: depart from me, ye that work iniquity."* The prophet Joseph Smith, in the Inspired Version of the Bible changes the above verse slightly. Instead of "I never knew you," the prophet changes it to "Ye never knew me." This is an important distinction. It is clear from these verses that many do not understand the difference between His works and our works because if they did, they would indeed know Him.

Those that fail to distinguish between the works inspired by our Lord and those they call "wonderful works," even casting out devils, which are inspired by seeking for a reward will not ever come to know Him, despite their protestations to the contrary. From the above, we have learned that the only works that produce celestial results are those that reflect the "will of my Father which is in heaven." All works done that do not reflect the will of our Heavenly Father are not justifiable. That doesn't mean that every good work is rejected as not being meritorious, but we are seeking justified works, which are by definition celestial works. They are works that the Spirit can seal and consecrate to us, those that reflect the will of our Heavenly Father. Thus, the question you are really asking is this: what must we do that will both enhance His work while at the same time justify our works consistent with the doctrine of justification which we have already discussed?

Let's begin at a new place to find out which works are deemed to be celestial works. We have already identified 2 Nephi 2 as one of the most important chapters of scripture because it sets the foundation for so many other doctrines. We now move on to two additional chapters that will prove to be "watershed" scriptures of profound meaning. These would be 2 Nephi 31 and 32. These chapters provide us a foundation, a basis, if you will, to answer the question of what **we should do and what we must allow the Lord to do.** This is fundamental to our proper understanding of our works and how the Lord brings to pass the Atonement in our own lives as well as in the lives of our investigators. Let's start by looking at 2 Nephi 31:19-21, *"And now, my beloved brethren, after ye have gotten into this strait and narrow path, I would ask if all is done? Behold, I say unto you, Nay; for ye have not come thus far save it were by the word of Christ* **with unshaken faith in him, relying wholly upon the merits of him who is mighty to save.** *Wherefore, ye must press forward with a steadfastness in Christ, having a perfect brightness of hope, and a love of God and of all men. Wherefore, if ye shall press forward,* ***feasting*** *upon the word of Christ, and endure to the end, behold, thus saith the Father: Ye shall have eternal life. And now, behold, my beloved brethren, this is the way; and there is* **none other way nor name given under heaven** *whereby man can be saved in the kingdom of God. And now, behold, this is the doctrine of Christ, and the only and true doctrine of the Father, and of the Son, and of the Holy Ghost..."*

We see then from this scripture how the relationship between our works and those of the Lord are segregated. Once again we clearly see that we must rely wholly on the Savior's works for our works to be valid. We read the same idea from passages in

Ephesians, Romans and Hebrews. I know that so far you are with me because we have already discussed the doctrine of grace and justified works; it was the grace of God that gave us the gifts of agency and faith, and therefore it is the grace of God that is upholding us and allowing us a probationary period to learn from our mistakes. Thus we are clear that it is the Savior's works upon which we must rely for our own salvation, and one of the greatest gifts that we eagerly receive comes to us as a result of His works; the gift of grace. The above verse makes this abundantly clear. It also makes clear that we must rely on the Savior's works **with unshaken faith** pressing forward with the brightness of hope and a love of God and of all mankind. These conditions of unshaken faith and a love for God and of all mankind are absolute prerequisites for any work done that reflects the will of our Father in heaven.

Unshaken faith must be developed and allowed to grow through the exercise of even a particle of faith as shown in Alma 32. So, if we truly trust Him, as we have learned before, bringing forth a broken heart and a contrite spirit so that faith and not pride will be developed through our works. Then our works will be done according to the will of our Heavenly Father and will be of a celestial nature as described in Section 88 of the Doctrine and Covenants quoted above. We have brought forth the very conditions which allow faith to be present as we, act to do our Heavenly Father's will. The second condition, shown in 2 Nephi 31 quoted above is that of love; love for God and for all mankind is an absolute prerequisite so that pride can be avoided. The Savior taught this with great passion in Matthew 22:36-40 as he responded to the question, *"Master, which is the great commandment in the law? Jesus said unto him, Thou shalt love the Lord thy God with all thy heart, and with all thy soul, and with all thy mind. This is the first and great commandment. And the second is like unto it, Thou shalt love thy neighbor as thyself.* **On these two commandments hang all the law and the prophets.**" The Savior basically told us, just as Nephi did, that we must press forward in unshaken faith with a love of God and of all mankind, for upon these conditions are justified works dependent.

Why is this so? If our works are not done out of our love of God and of our fellowman and if they are not done in faith, are they not good works? Is it not better to do any good thing, even if we have not faith or even if they are done in such a way that furthers our own cause? To answer this, let's turn to 2 Nephi 32:2-3 and 5, we read, *"Do ye not remember that I said unto you that after ye had received the Holy Ghost ye could speak with the tongue of angels? And now, how could ye speak with the tongue of angels save it were by the Holy Ghost? Angels speak by the power of the Holy Ghost; wherefore, they speak the words of Christ. Wherefore, I said unto you, feast upon the words of Christ; for behold, the words of Christ will tell you all things what ye should do...For behold, again I say unto you that if ye will enter in by the way, and receive the Holy Ghost, it will show unto you all things what ye should do."* If our works are not done under the direction of the Spirit, even though they are works that produce good results, they are not sealed upon us and hence are not justified. We must therefore feast upon the words of Christ, the scriptures, when we have received the gift of the Holy Ghost as we are confirmed after baptism, and as we read the scriptures and begin to use this wonderful gift, then a magnificent, even breathtaking event begins to occur. He, even the Lord Himself, through the Holy Ghost, will tell us what to do. He will put us in the position to receive inspiration to know how we should act, even with virtue and truth.

There is a great dynamic at work here in these two chapters of 2 Nephi that resolves the tension of the dialectic between faith and works and thereby sets parameters for understanding the difference between the Lord's work and our justified works. It is in understanding this dynamic that the tension is fully resolved. So, why do we begin here? In order to understand how we perform justified works, we first must press forward in a perfect hope, having faith in Christ so as to make the right decisions as to what work we should do. This establishes the dynamic of resolution: without faith, as we have already learned, we can do nothing to please God. Moreover, our works, while even mighty and good, if not done with faith secured through the love of God and our fellowman will not be justified.

Next, as a point of departure for our works, as established in the next part of the dynamic, we must do something to accept the gifts of salvation and exaltation made available to us by listening to the Spirit, for the Spirit "will tell us all things that we shall do." So, if we don't follow the first part of the dynamic, bringing forth our gifts of a broken heart and a contrite spirit so that we can obtain faith, we are not in a position to establish the second part of the dynamic, the performance of justified works. We inevitably will fall into the "activity trap," believing that we are "earning" our blessings instead of receiving them. By the way, it is difficult to earn a gift, but by receiving them with gratitude, and by basing our efforts on that gratitude, we both acknowledge that salvation and exaltation are gifts wrought by the work of the Savior and thereby we avoid pride. This validates Paul's statement that we are saved by faith, without the works of the law.

You may ask, "How do I avoid the 'activity trap' and perform justifiable or celestial works?" As I have explained before, many think they must "earn" the Lord's favor by doing great and important deeds. They feel they must do great things of themselves so that the Lord will love them and deliver to them the victory (or baptisms or leadership positions, or anything that brings worldly acclaim). But let me ask you, what did you do to "earn" your current leadership assignment, be it a district leader, zone leader or senior companion? Do you feel that your works were superior to those of your brethren? Of course not. The idea is silly. I know you are probably looking at yourself and saying, I didn't do anything to "earn" this job, and you would be right! No one in your district, zone or mission was asked to submit a resume; no one was given a "leadership test;" no, you were called to your current assignment, by those in authority through the Spirit of inspiration. The Lord has His reasons for your call, and it has nothing to do with "earning" it or being more "deserving" than other missionaries. He loves all of the missionaries in your district equally and wants all of you to succeed. You are not necessarily smarter, more spiritual, or in any way more qualified or better than anyone else in your district and I know you will agree with this. You have talents and abilities, as do the other members of your district. You have learned from others in your district and they have learned from you; you are all equal in the eyes of the Lord (see Romans 2:11).

So, why did the Lord call you, if it was not because you were more righteous or better, or in any way superior to your companions? Well, for right now, the Lord wants you to use the talents He has given you to serve Him. If we don't serve with faith and meekness, loving God and our fellowman, we run the great risk of developing the sin of pride. How do we use our talents to magnify Him? If we are sufficiently contrite through the development of a broken heart, and if we feel great love for the Lord and for our fellowman, we are able to move beyond the conditions established in this letter as prerequisites to justified works. We do this in two ways. First, we serve Him by keeping His commandments and second, by serving our fellow man; in your case, by serving the missionaries over whom He has given you responsibility concerning their welfare. You are to minister unto them as He would if He were there. This is a temporary call, just like almost all callings in the Church, and one day it will be given to another. You may have been given a leadership position at the MTC, in which case, it is a good time to ask yourself this question? What is it that the Lord will have you do? How do you employ the dynamic of doing works in faith, relying on the merits of the Lord, and doing the right works, inspired by the Spirit, which allows them to be justified?

As we have previously discussed, it is the Spirit that justifies our works, not the deeds of the law (2 Nephi 2:5-8). Now we will identify some key principles that will help you identify the kinds of works that can be justified. We begin with King Benjamin's address. In Mosiah 2:21 and part of verse 22 we read, *"I say unto you that if ye should **serve** him who has created you from the beginning, and is preserving you from day to day, by lending you breath, that ye may live and move and do according to your own will, and even supporting you from one moment to another – I say, if **ye should serve him with all your whole souls yet ye would be unprofitable servants.** And behold, all that he requires of you is to keep his commandments..."* We see from the above that our works, no matter how great they are still render us unprofitable servants. These verses reinforce what I said unto you in the previous six letters that our works are never comparable with His works. Then, from the above, what has He asked us to do? First, he has asked us to **keep** His commandments.

We may respond, "Well, this seems trite and general in meaning and does not tell us what specifically we should do." I might add that keeping His commandments with faith, meaning with a broken heart and a contrite spirit, in meekness is no easy task. If we keep his commandments, we show that we accept his gifts and are not trying to earn them. If we keep his commandments, he explains in the rest of verse 22 and then further in verses 23-25, *"...he has promised you that if ye would keep his commandments ye should prosper in the land; and he never doth vary from that which he hath said; therefore, if ye do keep his commandments he doth bless you and prosper you. And now, in the first place, he hath created you, and granted unto you your lives, for which ye are indebted unto him. And secondly, he doth require that ye should do as he hath commanded you; for which if ye do, he doth immediately bless you; and therefore he hath paid you. And ye are still indebted unto him, and are, and will be, forever and ever; therefore, of what have ye to boast? And now I ask, can ye say aught of yourselves? I answer you, Nay. Ye cannot say that ye are even as much as the dust of the earth; yet ye were created of the dust of the earth; but behold, it belongeth to him who created you."*

What this tells us is that we are **never** out of His debt because we are immediately blessed when we keep His commandments, if we do so **in meekness and humility, striving to develop unshaken faith in Him**, and not in our own abilities. Why is this so? It is because of the second part of the dynamic regarding our works. If we are obedient in humility and meekness, and are bringing forth the broken heart and contrite spirit which are the building blocks of faith and thereby allowing the Spirit to come into our lives, then the works we do will be justified and we will be able to receive the inspiration we need so that we might understand "all things that we must do." Now we return to that great chapter with which we began this letter. In 2 Nephi 31:12-13 and 17 we read, *"And also, the voice of the Son came unto me, saying: He that is baptized in my name, to him will the Father give the Holy Ghost,* **like unto me;** *wherefore,* **follow me, and do the things which ye have**

seen me do. *Wherefore, my beloved brethren, I know that if ye shall follow the Son, with **full purpose of heart, acting no hypocrisy and no deception before God,** but with real intent, repenting of your sins, witnessing unto the Father that ye are **willing** to take upon you the name of Christ, by baptism, - yea, by following your Lord and your Savior down into the water, according to his word, behold, then shall ye receive the Holy Ghost…Wherefore, do the things which I have told you I have seen your Lord and your Redeemer should do; for, for this cause have they been shown unto me, that ye might know the gate by which ye should enter. For the gate by which ye should enter is repentance and baptism by water; and then cometh a remission of your sins by fire and by the Holy Ghost."*

All right, we now must ask ourselves, what do these verses tell us about works? They tell us that the first thing we must do then, the first work that is to be justified is our baptism. I know you are now saying to me, "This is elementary; I was baptized when I was a child so why do we make such a big deal out of that?" The reason is that the conditions of baptism are fundamental to receiving the Spirit and it is the Spirit that justifies our works. Baptism is an introductory ordinance required by God in which He makes a covenant with those that are baptized that they may receive his Spirit. The Bible teaches that clearly. In Mark 16:16 we read, "*He that believeth and **is baptized** shall be saved; but he that believeth not shall be damned.*" The Bible also teaches us the correct manner of baptism. Paul taught the Romans (Romans 6:3-11), "*Know ye not, that so many of us as were baptized into Jesus Christ were baptized into his death? Therefore we are buried with him by baptism into death: that like as Christ was raised up from the dead by the glory of the Father, even so we also should walk in newness of life. For if we have been planted together in the likeness of his death, we shall be also in the likeness of his resurrection: Knowing this, that our old man is crucified with him, that the body of sin might be destroyed, that henceforth we should not serve sin. For he that is dead is freed from sin. Now if we be dead with Christ, we believe that we shall also live with him: Knowing that Christ being raised from the dead dieth no more; death hath no more dominion over him. For in that he died, he* *died unto sin once: but in that he liveth, he liveth unto God. Likewise reckon ye also yourselves to be dead indeed unto sin, but alive unto God through Jesus Christ our Lord."*

We learn from the previous verses two primary principles. First, (a Mormon myth debunked) that the waters of baptism do not remit the sins. We do not leave the sins we have in the water, but the water opens the gate as we make a covenant with the Lord and as we honor that covenant, by developing unshaken faith in Him and by loving God and our fellowman, the Holy Ghost remits our sins. We renew this covenant every time we partake of the sacrament. In the prayers offered for the bread and water, we find these words (Doctrine and Covenants 20:77), *"O God, the Eternal Father, we ask thee in the name of thy Son, Jesus Christ, to bless and sanctify this bread to the souls of all those who partake of it, that they may eat in remembrance of the body of thy Son, and witness unto thee, O God, the Eternal Father, that they are willing to take upon them the name of thy Son, and always remember him and keep his commandments which he has given them; that they may always have his Spirit to be with them. Amen."*

When I was a young Aaronic Priesthood holder, in 1962, President David O. McKay came to our ward to dedicate a new stake center. I was just becoming very interested in the gospel and its doctrines. As I was in the front of the chapel and during the sacrament service, I watched President McKay as he partook of the bread and water. It is through the ordinance of the sacrament that our baptismal covenant is renewed and by partaking of the sacrament, our lives are also renewed and are justified every week. Since I was then new to really knowing the gospel, I was acutely aware of President McKay's behavior. As the deacon passed the tray of bread to him and he selected a piece, he did not place the piece of bread immediately into his mouth. He looked at it, and as he looked, tears came to his eyes as he quietly contemplated the immense value of the sacrament of which he was about to partake. He realized what was going to happen as he worthily partook of the bread and water. My realization of the importance of the sacrament was complete. I **never** have taken the sacrament the same way again.

As you can see, the baptismal prayer provides the link to the covenant of baptism so that our works can be justified; the key to justification is that the Lord's Spirit will always be with us. If this justification happens, then our works will be of a celestial nature as defined in Section 88 of the Doctrine and Covenants, noted earlier. Therefore we baptize children at eight years old, not because they have sins (see Moroni 8:11), but because we want them to make a covenant with the Lord that when they do have sins, upon conditions of repentance, the Lord will remit them by the power of the Holy Ghost. We further see that without an authorized baptism we cannot be justified, no matter how good our works are. Baptism is the gateway to justified or celestial works. Without it, our works will either be terrestrial or telesial, meaning that if they are works that brought about "the good," they reflect the goodness of our soul and of course, they inure to our good as well. However, the good works to which the scriptures refer (see Alma 7:23-24) are celestial works. These then are the works that can be justified by the Holy Spirit of promise. This means they can be sealed by the Holy Ghost, which can only occur when we have been baptized by a priesthood holder who has been authorized so to do. With our confirmation, we receive the Gift of the Holy Ghost, which then allows our good works to be justified. Justified works live on after we are dead as they testify to our correct motives, that of desiring the kind of life that God Himself lives, eternal life. That is why the great work for the dead has been undertaken. Without baptism for the dead, those who lived on the earth that did not have an opportunity for such a baptism could not be justified before God.

Second, when we now look at the verse in 2 Nephi 31 along with the Bible verses, we learn what we are to do. Follow the Savior in our works, His works being an example to us. If we do so, we will receive the Holy Ghost (as He did), and our works will then be justified (as His works were). What kind of works will they be? Well, works that the Spirit inspires us to do, works that will be in tune with the mind and will of God. He obviously would not inspire us to commit adultery or steal or do rebellious and contentious deeds. These things cannot be justified. He obviously would not have us just sit around and do nothing. Remember, we will be judged by **our works** to see if these works conform to the will of our Heavenly Father and are confirmed and justified by His spirit. We know that works our prophet tells us to do are examples of the works that the Lord has commanded us to do; works such as going on a mission, or going to the temple; works that lengthen our stride. Specifically, we must feast on the words of Christ by reading the scriptures, for they too will tell us all things that we need to do.

All of the things we are commanded to do, as a result of our valid baptism, are works that can be justified, and by doing them, the Spirit causes these works to change us and transform us more properly into a person that is born again, as Paul suggested, in Romans 6:3-11. Paul's words suggest we put off the image of the world and be reborn through baptism in the image of our Savior. The sacrament is a "touchstone" event each week where we can examine ourselves (see 1 Corinthians 11:24-28) and see if the image of the Savior is still in our countenances (see Alma 5:14). A parent of a young missionary (who gets it) serving in El Salvador shared the following from her missionary son:

> I am grateful for my baptism and the unspeakable gift of the Holy Ghost. I am grateful for the Melchizedek priesthood I hold. I am grateful for the Endowment of power which I have received in the temple and for my testimony of the resurrected Savior and of the divine calling of the prophet Joseph Smith, through which Christ restored His gospel and [His] authority on the earth...I cannot and dare not deny them [the Father and the Son] because their light and truth have expanded my soul. I know that Jesus Christ is our Savior. He is risen. If we confess and repent of our sins, and strive to take the holy sacrament worthily every week, we will be found with Him in His kingdom. (copy of this letter is in the author's possession.)

The question of what works we are to do has now been answered. The next question is: how are we to perform these works? The example I will cite here comes from General Priesthood meeting many years ago. It was when President Benson counseled families in the church who had young children at home. He asked them if they could not restructure budgets in such a way so that mothers, who are indispensible to the lives of their young children, could spend more time with them. The Lord's prophet was giving families with younger children still at home good counsel. Since my wife died when we had young children at home, I did continually miss her influence with our children. The Lord did compensate as we discovered great nannies for the children, but oh, how we missed our mother! We now come to the fundamental question: How were families with young children to respond to the prophet's counsel? Many ignored the prophet and said, without faith, "We don't see the relevance of this statement and won't be obedient. We just won't follow him. He is an old man and out of touch with reality." Others, in acts of blind obedience, simply quit their jobs and suffered tremendous economic side effects which then caused them to blame the Lord and the prophet for their troubles. In both of these instances, the people did not **do** the works of the Savior. They did not follow Him.

If we take a family in the first group, it is obvious they did not follow the Lord. When they refused to follow the Lord's prophet, they lost the Spirit, which is the vital ingredient in **doing** the works the Lord has given us to do. If we take a family in group two, they, likewise, lost the Spirit. They never bothered to inquire of the Lord to receive "light and knowledge" on how they were to be obedient. They simply thought "in self righteousness" they would be blessed because they **acted on their own and relied on their own works.** This is a big problem among many in our church. How does the Lord want His works to be done? In the case of the second group, He would hope that these families, in faith, would go to Him and "wait upon Him" as Isaiah 40:31 suggests and let Him answer their prayers showing them "how" they should be obedient. This isn't listening to others and having them tell the family what they "should" do; this is the family itself relying wholly on the Lord and committing to follow what the Lord tells them. If they had done this, I know they would find justification for their actions and through this, their faith would increase because they would have relied on the Lord.

What have we learned so far about works? Well, we have learned that the only works that become celestial works are those that conform to the will of our Heavenly Father. Those kinds of works are illustrated by the baptismal covenant. The first principles and ordinances of the gospel are, first faith in the Lord Jesus Christ (the first law of heaven), second, repentance (meaning turning around our behavior through sincere godly sorrow), third, baptism by immersion administered by one having authority and fourth, receiving (not earning) the gift of the Holy Ghost. The pattern outlined in 2 Nephi 31 and 32 then continues as we partake of the sacrament and renew this first and primary covenant with the Lord. As we make additional covenants, partaking of the sacrament also renews them; it is the ordinance of the sacrament after we are baptized that conveys the Spirit to us and justifies the works done according to the promptings of the Spirit, often outlined by our prophets.

Does the Lord confirm what I just said to you? Yes, He does. In Doctrine and Covenants 52:14-19, He confirms this pattern established in the way He has told us to follow Him, *"And again, I will give unto you a pattern in all things, that ye may not be deceived; for Satan is abroad in the land, and he goeth forth deceiving the nations – Wherefore he that prayeth, whose **spirit is contrite**, the same is accepted of me **if he obey mine ordinances**. He that speaketh, whose spirit is contrite, whose language is meek and edifieth, the same is of God **if he obey mine ordinances**. And again, he that trembleth under my power shall be made strong, and shall bring forth fruits of praise and wisdom, according to the revelations and truths which I have given you. And again, he that is overcome and bringeth not forth fruits, even according to this pattern, **is not of me**. Wherefore, by this pattern, ye shall know the spirits in all cases under the whole heavens."* The tension between faith, grace and works is resolved in this pattern as shown above.

Nephi taught us that as we prepare to make a covenant with the Lord, He would send us the Holy Ghost; once the covenant has been made, we must continue to follow the pattern of His as set forth in the scriptures and according to the pattern shown in the previous paragraph. The conditions of a broken heart and a contrite spirit are always a requirement in doing any work because they are the building blocks of faith. With them, and if we obey the ordinances we have undertaken, His Spirit will justify these works and they will be counted as celestial works that rise with us in the resurrection of the dead. Unjustified works are of no effect after men are dead. I think I would like to offer you an example from the scriptures of the doctrine we have just established.

In John 11:19-43, long passages I grant you, we see in the raising of Lazarus from the dead, how this pattern works. We read, *"And many of the Jews came to Martha and Mary, to comfort them concerning their brother. Then Martha, as soon as she heard that Jesus was coming, went and met him: but Mary sat still in the house. Then said Martha unto Jesus, Lord, if thou hadst been here, my brother had not died. But I know, that even now, whatsoever thou wilt ask of God, God will give it thee. Jesus saith unto her, Thy brother shall rise again. Martha saith unto him, I know that he shall rise again in the resurrection at the last day. Jesus said unto her, I am the resurrection, and the life: he that believeth in me, though he were dead, yet shall he live: And whosoever liveth and believeth in me shall never die. Believest thou this? She saith unto him, Yea, Lord: I believe that thou art the Christ, the Son of God, which should come into the world. And when she had so said, she went her way, and called Mary her sister secretly, saying, The Master is come, and calleth for thee. As soon as she heard that, she arose quickly, and came unto him. Now Jesus was not yet come into the town, but was in that place where Martha met him. The Jews then which were with her in the house, and comforted her, when they saw Mary, that she rose up hastily and went out, followed her, saying, She goeth unto the grave to weep there."*

I know we are just getting into these verses and they will make sense in a minute, so bear with me as we continue, *"Then when Mary was come where Jesus was, and saw him, she fell down at his feet, saying unto him, Lord, if thou hadst been here, my brother had not died. When Jesus therefore saw her weeping, and the Jews also weeping which came with her, he groaned in the spirit, and was troubled, And said, Where have ye laid him? They said unto him, Lord, come and see.*

Jesus wept. Then said the Jews, Behold how he loved him! And some of them said, Could not this man, which opened the eyes of the blind, have caused that even this man should not have died? Jesus therefore again groaning in himself cometh to the grave. It was a cave, and a stone lay upon it. Jesus said, Take ye away the stone. Martha, the sister of him that was dead, saith unto him, Lord, by this time he stinketh: for he hath been dead four days. Jesus saith unto her, Said I not unto thee, that, if thou wouldest believe, thou shouldest see the glory of God? Then they took away the stone from the place where the dead was laid. And Jesus lifted up his eyes, and said, Father, I thank thee that thou hast heard me. And I knew that thou hearest me always: but because of the people which stand by I said it, that they may believe that thou hast sent me. And when he thus had spoken, he cried with a loud voice, Lazarus, come forth."

Well, after such a long recitation of scripture, what does all of this illustrate? We see the response of the Savior to the death of his friend Lazarus as well as the response of his sisters, Mary and Martha to Lazarus' death as well. These interactions are illustrative of the pattern discussed in Doctrine and Covenants 52 and thereby we see how the tension between grace, faith and works is resolved by the very application of that pattern. First of all, we see the love of God and all mankind illustrated by the Savior as well as by Mary and Martha. We see the Jews that were with them also loved Mary and Martha and were eager to believe. So let us now contrast the response to Jesus' visit by Martha first and Mary second. Martha runs to the Savior and I am certain upbraids Him just a little for not being there to save Lazarus. Mary, in contrast, waited upon the Lord, just as Isaiah had taught us (see Isaiah 40:*31*). It was clear that Martha, while believing the words of the Savior did not completely understand them. Remember, she was the sister who was so encumbered by getting everything cleaned up when the Savior had come to dinner (Luke 10:41-42), the Savior gently rebuked Martha when he said, "*...Martha, Martha, thou art careful and troubled about many things: But one thing is needful: and Mary hath chosen that good part, which shall not be taken away from her.*" Do you see the difference between their approaches? Martha was still too busy and did not wait for the Lord to call her; was too encumbered (by programs, meetings, or the like) to truly wait for the Lord to speak to her heart.

Thus, Martha was still troubled about many things when her brother died. She boldly went forth to meet the Savior and give him a little piece of her mind. When he tried to bring vision to her complaint, she demonstrated that she understood the doctrine of the resurrection, but did not appreciate the purpose of His visit. Mary, on the other hand, waited upon the Lord until the Lord asked to see her. She, unlike Martha, approached the Lord with a broken heart and a contrite spirit. Why do we know this? Because she knelt before him and in a tone, I believe much different than that of Martha, asked the Lord the same question. Because she approached the Lord in meekness, and in faith, note the Savior's response, He "groaned" within himself – the effects of Mary's faith were self-evident. With the contrite spirit, Mary was able to pray in faith and importune the Lord consistent with His own desires. She knew the will of the Father as reflected in the will of the Son; and because she had a contrite spirit her faith was made powerful and unshakable. She had the Lord's attention and she did not waste His precious time in puzzle solving. She desired the Lord to raise her brother from the dead and her faith, mixed with His desire activated a powerful force and produced the desired effect. The Lord spoke the words, "Lazarus come forth" and under these circumstances, is there any doubt that he would? No, of course not.

There is one final matter we need to discuss within the context of our works versus the Savior's works. As this letter has shown, our works are inferior to His works, but still, there is the matter of 2 Nephi 25:23 which states, *"For we labor diligently to write, to persuade our children, and also our brethren, to believe in Christ, and to be reconciled to God; for we know that it is by grace we are saved, after all we can do."* This verse has created some confusion about the relationship between faith, grace and works and has heightened the tension between them, which we discussed early on in this letter. Let me say categorically, that we are saved by grace, period. Without the Lord's grace, we cannot in any way be saved. Are we saved without the works of the law as Paul suggests in Romans? As we have already shown, the answer to that question is, yes. What of works then? Well, as we have shown, the key to this conundrum is found in James 2:22, *"Seest thou how faith wrought with his works, and by works was faith made perfect?"* Works make our faith perfect because they demonstrate that we will accept His great gift of salvation. I think what brother Joseph Fielding McConkie has written on this subject is of great interest here. I discussed this subject with him personally back in 2002 when he came to Salt Lake to teach a class within our stake. He has since passed away, but we got along fine and although we disagreed on certain points of doctrine, on this one we were together. The following quote reflects our conversation:

> During my growing up years in the Church, I cannot remember a single Sunday School, priesthood, or seminary lesson on the subject of grace. Nor do I remember anyone speaking on the matter in sacrament meeting. Grace was generally thought to be a Protestant doctrine, and Latter-day Saints knew that all blessings were predicated upon obedience to gospel laws....What is most embarrassing about all this is that I was completely ignorant that the doctrine of Christ's grace is one of the great themes of the Book of Mormon....Martin Luther would have loved the Book of Mormon. (*Straightforward Answers to Tough Gospel Questions* pages 59-62.)

What Lehi says (2 Nephi 2:5) is that our obedience to the laws and ordinances of the gospel will not save us. Law is not our Savior. God ordained the laws; the laws did not ordain God. Yet even if we were foolish enough to suppose that the power of salvation was to be found in the laws, we still couldn't be saved because none of us could be justified by the law. That is, the law could not acquit us; it could not find us innocent because we have all sinned and fallen short of the demands of the law. Lehi further said in verses 6-7, *"Wherefore, redemption cometh in and through the Holy Messiah; for he is full of grace and truth. Behold, he offereth himself a sacrifice for sin, to answer the ends of the law...*" Now note this plain and precious declaration – "*unto all who have a broken heart and a contrite spirit; and unto none else can the ends of the law be answered.*" The doctrine is perfect. It needs no tailoring to fit comfortably alongside the necessity of individual responsibility. There is no cheap grace here.

So, again, let's put this into proper context. We are saved by the Savior's works, not our works. Why? Because His works are so much greater than our works, they are not on the same level at all. So a few additional verses provide final clarification. In Alma 7:24 the context between grace and works is clarified and in this context, the tension is resolved, "*And see that ye have faith, hope, and charity,* **AND THEN** *ye will always abound in good works.*" This of course means justified works. Then what about this business of all we can do? Aren't we supposed to do most of the work so the Savior can make up the difference? This is rubbish. He does ALL the work of salvation and exaltation; it is His works, which are superior to our works that makes salvation and exaltation possible. Our works are present to put us in a position to accept His work. That is why Lamoni's brother, Anti-Nephi-Lehi stated so emphatically in Alma 24:11, "*And now behold, my brethren, since it has been all that we could do (as we were the most lost of all mankind) to repent of all our sins and the many murders which we have committed, and to get God to take them away from our hearts, for it was all we could do to repent sufficiently before God that he would take away our stain.*" Often, all we can do is bring forth a broken heart and a contrite spirit, the only requirements to have the ends of the law answered upon us, and then repent and keep His commandments; following Him in every way through the waters of baptism so that we may receive the gift of the Holy Ghost. With that gift, the Holy Spirit of promise can make our works celestial through the doctrine of justification by the Spirit.

I hope your question about our works versus the Savior's works has been answered. Let us acknowledge, even with great gratitude, the grace of our Lord in granting us agency; let us thank him abundantly for staying His mighty hand and granting to us a probationary state during which we may learn and repent of our many sins. Finally, let us bring this great message of the restoration of the gospel as an example of His great and wonderful grace to the children of our Heavenly Father with diligence and with the dignity it deserves. I know you will be a fine example to those you will teach of humility, meekness, and charity. Rejoice with them as they realize the power of the works of the Savior in bringing to pass their salvation and possible exaltation.

With deep personal regards for the sanctity and importance of your calling,

LETTER EIGHT

WHAT IS THE RELATIONSHIP BETWEEN FAITH, KNOWLEDGE, AND OBEDIENCE?

The Missionary Training Center is a perfect place to learn about the relationship between faith, knowledge, and obedience. As we become more capable of learning by the Spirit, we come to understand the power of faith; this power brings us knowledge and strengthens our desires to be obedient.

Dear Missionary,

  I sure did enjoy hearing from you and I am pleased to know that the discussions on grace, agency and justified works are beginning to make sense. You now see that although the MTC takes a little getting-used to, your efforts there are beginning to bear fruit. You must realize that the Missionary Training Center is the only way that the Brethren could train so many missionaries at one time. So please continue to have an honest attitude about the MTC, which allows you to take the much good it has to offer and reject that "stuff" which is bizarre and not of the Spirit. You are learning that humility and meekness is a great attribute, which allows you to access spiritual or transcendental realms. It is in these realms that ultimate certitude about God and His work is to be found. You have so many gifts and abilities and these are only enhanced as you become more humble and meek. After all, as these traits grow in us, our ability to bring forth the sacrifice of a broken heart and a contrite spirit is enhanced (see Doctrine and

Covenants 59:8).

As we bring forth these sacrifices, actually gifts to the Lord, we know we receive the gift of faith (1 Corinthians 12:9). With faith, all things are possible to God. It is here we will begin our next discussion of faith and how it relates to obedience and the acquisition of knowledge. We will discover that, like agency, grace and justified works are interdependent principles, so too are faith, obedience and the acquisition of knowledge through the Spirit. As we have previously learned, the place to begin to understand this interdependence begins with faith, as faith is the first principle of the gospel. We will learn that we must receive the gift of faith by bringing forth a broken heart and a contrite spirit as a prerequisite to our obedience.

Elder Bruce R. McConkie has written in *Mormon Doctrine* that "obedience is the first law of heaven" and this is often quoted out of context. Elder McConkie never meant to imply that obedience is blind and precedes faith. Unfortunately, we in the church often emphasize obedience, even hyper-obedience, as a principle that is both blind and preferred to faith. The only way that obedience is the "first law of heaven" is if it conforms to what the Prophet Joseph Smith has written in the "Articles of Faith." The very first article tells us that the first principle (or law) of heaven is faith. Paul tells us in Hebrews 11:6 that without faith, "*it is impossible to please him (God).*" Further, in Doctrine and Covenants 8:10, "*That without faith, you can do nothing...*" Therefore, as we have demonstrated in the prior seven letters, when men are not sufficiently humble, they don't have the ability to receive the gift of faith and thus they sometimes act strangely. True obedience flows from faith because we wish to have the Lord's Spirit with us; if we have not received the gift of faith, often times our obedience is mere conformity. When we are conformant, our reasons for such behavior can be linked to blindness; we conform in a rote manner, without feeling or thought for Him who commands our obedience. We become habitual in our behavior as a matter of routine. We must be careful that this conformity is not viewed as a substitute for true obedience, which is sighted and enlightening.

For example, there was a missionary in the Language Training Mission (a precursor to the MTC) who delighted in coming up to people with whom he disagreed and would say stupid things like, "The Spirit told me you are wrong." I have marveled at such a lack of knowledge of how the Spirit works and how we are really empowered by Him. It soon became clear to me that this brother actually *lacked* faith and was very prideful. He was trying to rely on his own merits and learning, not relying on the Lord and His knowledge. It is interesting to learn that the Spirit does not work that way at all. As an example, we can look back on the Mark Hoffman debacle of twenty-five years ago. Hoffman presented multiple forged documents to Presidents Kimball, Hinckley and Monson. Each of these brethren we sustain as Prophets, Seers and Revelators. These brethren didn't suddenly burst in on Mark Hoffman and say, "The Spirit just told me you are wrong!" In fact, the Lord has said just the opposite in Doctrine and Covenants 10:35-37: *"Marvel not that I said unto you: Here is wisdom, show it not unto the world – for I said, show it not unto the world, that you may be preserved. Behold, I do not say that you shall not show it unto the righteous...or as* **you cannot always tell the wicked from the righteous, therefore I say unto you, hold your peace until I shall see fit to make all things known unto the world concerning the matter."**

In fact, these brethren didn't know of the truth about Hoffman until the Lord Himself made all things concerning Hoffman known to the world. So, let's return back to my missionary friend. The Spirit just doesn't work the way this brother thought. He later learned that it was his arrogance, produced by blind obedience and faithless works that caused him to be easily deceived by Lucifer. He did repent, his heart did break and the Spirit made him into a good missionary. (Incidentally, the missionary to whom I am referring is me!). The quiet efforts of the Holy Ghost, found in small things, produce the best results and a rock-solid testimony. Boy, am I certainly grateful for these lessons. Yes, my dear friend, I know by sad, personal experience that faith is indeed the first law of heaven. It is obedience rendered in faith that counts, not just blind obedience. That is why I loved what you said just at the beginning of your letter. "The reason therefore that I am going on my mission; 1) humility, 2) humility, 3) humility." I needed to learn this lesson after I left to go into my field of labor; you have mastered it while yet at the Missionary Training Center. This is terrific!

I enjoyed so much your thoughts concerning being able to express your feelings. You said that you will be able to bear witness to the truth of the work through the Spirit, and because of your faith, love and desire to bring the truth of the gospel to those wonderful people, they too will feel the power of your words. In that regard, I love what Nephi said concerning Laman and Lemuel. His brothers did not feel the Spirit and were numb to it. They had long rejected their father's message, calling him a "visionary man" meant not as a compliment but as a rebuke. It was not logical to them that they should be forced out of Jerusalem into the wilderness. Thus, they refused to be "born again" by the Spirit, they refused to "see" the great work in which they had been asked to participate. They had to be humbled. Note Nephi's words (1 Nephi 17:45-46): *"Ye are swift to do iniquity but slow to remember the Lord your God. Ye have seen an angel, and he spake unto you; yea;* **ye have heard his voice from time to time; and he hath spoken unto you in a still small voice, but ye were past feeling, that ye could not feel his words;** *wherefore, he has spoken unto you like unto the voice of thunder, which did cause the earth to shake as if it were to divide asunder. And ye also know that by the power of his almighty word...he can cause the rough places to be made smooth, and smooth places shall be broken up. O, then, why is it, that ye can be so hard in your hearts?"*

Indeed, why were these brethren so hard in their hearts? It was because they were arrogant and proud. In Letter Five, we discussed the fact that pride, the universal sin came to them because of disobedience and the lack of belief in their father's words. As we have also previously noted, pride can also come because of hyper-obedience (blind obedience), which exalts such a person to think of themselves as superior over their brethren because they think they are "more learned," or "more prepared." In general, they think they are more highly favored of the Lord than everyone else. Paul wrote in Romans 3:9-12: *"What then? are we better than they? No, in no wise: for we have before proved both Jews and Gentiles, that they are all under sin; As it is written, There is none righteous, no, not one:* (see Luke 18:19 – Paul is quoting Jesus) *There is none that understandeth, there is none that seeketh after God. They are all gone out of the way, they are together become unprofitable; there is none that doeth good, no, not one."* And again in Ecclesiastes 7:20, *"For there is not a just* [justified] *man upon the earth, that doeth good, and sinneth not."* It truly pays to be humble and not to try to use "bashing" to teach truth. It does not invite the Spirit.

You know I love philosophy, and it is a useful tool in many circumstances, after all, it is part of my Ph.D. When teaching the truths of the gospel to non-members, its use can be tempting, but it is a "heady brew" that frequently produces arrogance completely inconsistent with the desires of the Spirit. It therefore must be subordinate to the scriptures and the words of the prophets. When we realize how privileged we are to be members of this church, to have access to the Holy Priesthood of God and on top of that, to be called to be His disciple and to preach the gospel; all of this overwhelms me and I am smitten with the truth that we know so very little compared to what God knows. As to our knowledge, we are but little children, in His words (Doctrine and Covenants 78:17). All that we have is true; but we do not have all the truth. There is much to be revealed and much to be learned. And it is to be learned by the power of faith as combined with our other spiritual gifts. What a task! How do we have time to be arrogant or prideful, especially in our obedience? These things profit us nothing.

This review concerning pride now serves as a point of departure for me to answer your questions. You asked me about faith and knowledge and the role of obedience in obtaining both. You referenced Doctrine and Covenants, section 46. This section, as you know, deals with spiritual gifts. As we know, all have spiritual gifts or at least one gift. These are manifest in differing degrees among us. Some of us have great faith, others knowledge. Still others have power to believe, while yet others have power to teach. All of these gifts mix in us to some degree or another, as each person is different (see 1 Corinthians 14). However, faith and knowledge go hand in hand, just like it says in Alma 32. We have to be careful here, because we just might encounter a "Mormon myth" concerning the relationship between the two. The myth goes something like this: "once I have used my faith to gain knowledge, I don't need faith anymore." Those who think this way often cite Alma 32:34, which tells us that faith is dormant and that if one has a perfect knowledge concerning the object of the faith (verse 34), faith itself is no longer needed. People who believe this cite as proof for that view the words found in Ether 3:19, which states: *"And because of the knowledge of this man he could not be kept from beholding within the veil; and he saw the finger of Jesus, which, when he saw, he fell with fear; for he knew that it was the finger of the Lord; and he had faith no longer, for he knew, nothing doubting."*

To infer from these two scriptures that faith will be replaced by knowledge is to reach beyond one's grasp. If this was so, then why do other scriptures state the role of faith differently? For example, concerning the role of faith, we read in 2 Corinthians 5:7, *"For we walk by faith, not by sight."* Further, we can look to the Doctrine and Covenants 8:10, *"without faith, ye can do nothing."* In addition, the Prophet Joseph Smith tells us that faith is a power, a gift more precious than knowledge. In the *Lectures on Faith*, Lecture 1, we read, "Faith is not only the principle of action, but of power also, in all intelligent beings, whether in heaven or on earth. Thus says the author of the epistle to the Hebrews, 11:3." Moreover, again in Lecture 1, we learn that faith is the power by which the worlds were created:

> Through faith we understand that the worlds were framed by the word of God; so that things which are seen were not made of things which do not appear. By this we understand that the principle of power which extended in the bosom of God, by which the worlds were framed, was faith; and that it is by reason of this principle of power existing in the Deity, that all created things exist; so that all things in heaven, on earth, or under the earth exist by reason of faith as it existed in Him. Had it not been for the principle of faith the worlds would never have been

framed neither would man have been formed of dust. It is the principle by which Jehovah works, and through which he exercises power over all temporal as well as eternal things. Take this principle or attribute – for it is an attribute -- from the Deity. (*Lectures on Faith* – Lecture 1:14-16.)

In Lecture 2, the prophet explains, "God is...omnipotent, omnipresent and **omniscient**; without beginning of days or end of life; and...in him the principle of faith dwells independently..." (*Lectures on Faith* – Lecture 2:2.) Finally, Moroni unequivocally explains the fact that faith is never superseded by anything when he wrote (Moroni 7:20 and 25-26): *"And now, my brethren, how is it possible that ye can lay hold upon every good thing? Wherefore, by the ministering of angels, and by every word which proceeded forth out of the mouth of God, men began to exercise faith in Christ; and thus **by faith**, they did lay hold upon every good thing; and thus it was until the coming of Christ. And after that he came men also were **saved by faith** in his name; and by faith, they become the sons of God. And as surely as Christ liveth he spake these words unto our fathers, saying: Whatsoever thing ye shall ask the Father in my name, which is good, **in faith** believing that ye shall receive, behold, it shall be done unto you."* If God has all knowledge, yet still has faith that should tell us all something. So, it appears from these verses that those who previously concluded, "I don't need faith anymore once I have knowledge," have concluded wrongly.

Let's see if we can't reconcile these two views. To begin, let's return to Alma 32 where those who believe that after we have knowledge, we don't need faith. Here we see that Alma gives us a clue. He says that the fruit of our faith is knowledge and that when such knowledge is obtained, our faith goes dormant; not that it goes away and is not needed any longer. Faith remains the glue that keeps this transcendental knowledge intact. The knowledge we have received through the exercise of faith would disappear if faith did not remain, even dormant faith. If we lose our faith by being arrogant and thinking faith is no longer necessary, we will in fact lose the knowledge gained through our faith. In other words, if we learn the things of God through faith, this transcendental knowledge so learned will become transient and relative should our faith no longer continue, even in a dormant state.

What are the first fruits of faith? Well, they are repentance and change. Once this change has occurred, or once knowledge gained by faith has obtained, what of our dormant faith? Here it is important to acknowledge that faith is still present, only dormant. If faith was no longer present, what would happen to that knowledge so obtained through it? I submit to you that faith is the foundation, the superstructure, if you will, of that knowledge. If faith were to be withdrawn, then the knowledge obtained through that faith would collapse. Faith prods us to grow to even greater levels of knowledge. What kind of knowledge does faith produce? It produces knowledge from the realms of heaven, transcendental realms that often do not intersect with the empirical world or the world of the senses.

This means that there are two kinds of knowledge. First, there is knowledge that can be apprehended by the senses – meaning sight, sound, and touch. The second kind of knowledge is that knowledge which is comprehended by the spirit; this means we use transcendental sources, self-evident sources, to obtain knowledge. It is only in this realm that certainty is obtainable. Why? Because knowledge obtained by the senses is never completely certain. We can say within a realm of probability that an observable event is true. We can never be 100 percent certain. Our senses can be deceived and as we obtain more knowledge under this method, our previous conclusions may change or may be found to be in error. With transcendental certitude, the only way this knowledge fails us, or changes, is when we lose our faith. If faith is taken away, the conclusions and truth we obtained though faith are blurred as the superstructure and foundation created by faith collapse. Faith can be dormant, but never absent.

As we now have defined two realms where truth can be obtained, and we have shown that when we gain knowledge by faith, we must nurture our faith so that it grows and becomes stronger. If we do this, the transcendental knowledge that has produced a certainty will become unmovable. If we don't nourish our faith, it can fail us; and with that failure, the knowledge so obtained though faith will also fail us. This is a root cause of apostasy and of the falling away that is mentioned prominently in the scriptures. So how do we nourish and strengthen our faith? In Luke 17, we begin to find the answer. In verses 5-10 we read: *"And the apostles said unto the Lord, Increase our faith. And the Lord said, If ye had faith as a grain of mustard seed, ye might say unto this sycamine tree, Be thou plucked up by the root, and be thou planted in the sea; and it should obey you. But which of you, having a servant plowing or feeding cattle, will say unto him by and by, when he is come from the field, Go and sit down to meat? And will not rather say unto him, Make ready wherewith I may sup, and gird thyself, and serve me, till I have eaten and drunken; and afterward thou shalt eat and drink? Doth he thank that servant because he did the things that were commanded him? I trow not.* **So likewise ye, when ye shall have done all those things which are commanded you, say, We are unprofitable servants: we have done that which was our duty to do."**

Notice that the Lord begins his answer to the apostles' inquiry about faith and how to increase it by saying if they had the faith of a mustard seed, they should be able to do great things. A mustard seed is tiny; so the Lord has reinforced what we have already discussed: by small things, great results are brought to pass. Remember further that the Lord's words are a response to the question, "How do we increase our faith?" Here the Lord tells them to do the things that they have been commanded to do and still call themselves "unprofitable." By calling themselves "unprofitable servants," he reminds them to continue to have a broken heart and a contrite spirit, for these are indispensable traits in not only receiving faith, but certainly increasing it. In addition, he explains that it is they that need to continue to serve the Lord until the Lord's needs are met, an absolute condition of the broken heart. They need to seek and to remain on the Lord's agenda, not their own. If they do this, their faith will increase **as a direct result from the knowledge they obtain by service to God.** Faith does not come to them in the form of an "earned" blessing, for it is a gift of God as we previously have noted. However, we see that once the gift of faith has been received by the bringing forth of a broken heart and a contrite spirit, the result of knowledge learned by that faith, is increased faith.

What of the faith used to produce this knowledge? Acts of service in the Lord's behalf produce certitude about His mission and His works. This certitude is not available by pursuing such truth through the senses. Such certainty comes from faith and even as the knowledge obtained through faith feeds the soul, it must remain to ensure the knowledge so obtained also remains. When faith has produced this incontrovertible assurance, it becomes dormant (as if sleeping), waiting to be again awakened, as it is needed. It will be indeed needed again, specifically to grow more firmly in our understanding of heavenly realms, which will enable us to find the confidence we need to seek truth. Let's go back to Alma 32. Here we see that Alma tells us to undertake an experiment with his words. He says that faith is not a perfect knowledge (but it is knowledge nonetheless – thus it is sighted, not blind). If we will but experiment with his words by planting them into our hearts like unto a seed, (even perhaps a mustard seed) and not cast them out, this is the first step. Why do we tend to cast them out? We do so when we nourish doubt because of unbelief. Doubt can be a very useful tool that insulates us from exaggerated acts done to prove our faith, but if we are not careful, then doubt will strangle the words we have planted. We need to nourish these words, like seeds, through justified works of the Spirit such as those done in the cause of Christ.

Then the words will swell within us and we will feel our faith begin to blossom into knowledge. If we continue to nourish the words so planted through faith, they will grow to a perfect state. The process will **strengthen and increase** our faith but will never render it unnecessary. Faith, in this process, becomes dormant, not dead. Alma tells us that only our knowledge of a particular "thing" is made perfect, not all of our knowledge. He then states in verse 36: *"Behold I say unto you, Nay; neither must ye lay aside your faith, for ye have only exercised your faith to plant the seed that ye might try the experiment to know if the seed was good."*

To sum up then, we see from these verses that faith begets knowledge, even perfect knowledge of a particular "thing" which renders the faith to produce this knowledge dormant. Once this cycle is completed, and perfect knowledge obtained, then, as Alma suggests, the fruit of this knowledge is more faith. This reinforces Luke's account (Luke 17) of how to **increase** our faith. We see that Alma's process strengthens faith; Luke's account of continuing in a broken heart and a contrite spirit while doing the will of the Lord, **strengthens** our faith. Both accounts tell us that faith must continue to be an active part of our experience with the Lord, just as the scriptures cited above tell us. It is simply **not true** that once faith produces knowledge, that faith is no longer needed.

Indeed, the Prophet Joseph Smith was correct when he taught in the *Lectures on Faith,* that it was by the power of faith, the faith of the Lord Jesus Christ Himself that the worlds were created; the power through which the worlds came into being is a transcendental power, not an empirical power that exercised dominion over the elements. Faith in its perfect form reposes itself completely in the Lord. The Lord has perfect knowledge and perfect faith. These two act together to affect the power of creation and the power in the priesthood. Remember always it is by faith that we are healed; by faith we act in the name of the Lord; and it is by faith, the first principle of the gospel that the rest of the gospel, including knowledge, is brought forth. Faith is therefore truly the first law of heaven, not obedience. It was in faith that the Lord went to the cross, and by His faith was the work of salvation made perfect and the Atonement made real for us. I realize that in Doctrine and Covenants 130:20, the Lord told us, *"There is a law, irrevocably decreed in heaven before the foundations of this world, upon which all blessings are predicated."* Because I am a teacher, I note that there is but one law that is irrevocably decreed, not two or three or thousands. What is that law? I think the above has clearly established that nothing happens in the Lord's kingdom without faith, not even the creation.

You ask further, what about the next verse, verse 21, which states, *"And when we obtain any blessing from God, it is by obedience to that law upon which it is predicated."* Again the law upon which all blessings are predicated is the law of faith. This idea of "mixing and matching" blessings to being obedient to certain laws is childish. Of course certain blessings such as tithing for example, come with a promise that if such activity is undertaken, blessings will obtain. I must remind you however, that specific blessings are never attached to such promises. Undoubtedly, if we have a broken heart and a contrite spirit, we certainly don't "haggle" with the Lord over what blessings He will send us due to our obedience. When we are meek, we leave that up to Him. We know that He knows what we need and we trust Him to deliver (see Matthew 6:8). Through our faith and the pursuit of transcendental knowledge, we know with certitude that He will deliver. For we have come to know Him and we know that it is His nature to bless us because He loves us so completely and so unconditionally. As John has told us in 1 John 4:18-19, *"There is no fear in love; but perfect love casteth out fear: because fear hath torment. He that feareth is not made perfect in love.* **We love him because he first loved us.**" Trying to force the Lord's hand, as it were, and force Him to bless us according to our desires and not His, is unseemly and bespeaks a complete lack of faith in Him. All things must be done according to the law of faith, even obedience.

    Yes, my dear friend, faith is always necessary. Let's look at a last example concerning faith and obedience with the brother of Jared whose story is found in the Book of Mormon. In this example, Moroni relates the story of the brother of Jared. You will remember that because the brother of Jared asked, the Lord touched the stones he had fashioned so that the vessels used to cross the ocean would have light. Let's pick up the narrative after the brother of Jared saw the finger of the Lord. In Ether 3:9-13: *"And the Lord said unto him: Because of thy **faith** thou hast seen that I shall take upon me flesh and blood; and never has man come before me with such exceeding faith as thou hast; for were it not so ye could not have seen my finger. Sawest thou more than this? And he answered: Nay; Lord, show thyself unto me. And the Lord said unto him: **Believest** thou the words which I shall speak? And he answered: Yea, Lord, I **know** that thou speakest the truth, for thou art a God of truth, and canst not lie. And when he had said these words, behold, the Lord showed himself unto him, and said:*

*Because thou **knowest** these things ye are redeemed from the fall; therefore ye are brought back into my presence; therefore I show myself unto you."* What the brother of Jared said concerning faith was not that he did not need it any more, but that his faith brought the very presence of the Lord to him. Without faith, he couldn't have seen God. Was his faith then dormant? Yes it was, but if his faith was to falter, I am certain that even the knowledge he received through his faith would also falter.

Moroni, in his commentary in verse 19 said: *"And because of the knowledge of this man he could not be kept from beholding within the veil; and he saw the finger of Jesus, which, when he saw, he fell with fear; for he knew that it was the finger of the Lord; and he had faith no longer, for he knew, nothing doubting."* The knowledge was produced by faith and so perhaps the verse could be explained, "and he had active faith no longer, for he knew, nothing doubting and his faith had become dormant." The knowledge of this did not supersede his faith; to the contrary, it served to strengthen it, just as Alma suggests. Certainly some of it went dormant, but what he brought back was a faith that, in the words of Enos, who had a similar experience, began to be "unshakable" in the Lord (see Enos 1:11). This strengthening of his faith undoubtedly caused his heart to become even more broken and his spirit even more contrite. With this occurrence, he certainly counted himself an unprofitable servant for this knowledge had overcome him with his own sense of need to depend on the Lord. This is exactly what Luke's account said would happen. Thus, his faith also increased, not diminished because of his experience seeing the Lord.

Now, what about this business of faltering faith? I said above that if faith were to fail, what about the knowledge procured through faith? Would such knowledge also fail and go away? This was certainly true of Oliver Cowdery. As his faith collapsed, he lost his witness, and although he never denied what he had seen, he was not valiant in that testimony. As time passed and as his faith continued to wane, he was at first antagonistic to the church and its leaders; however, time also produced in Oliver a sense of perspective and proportion. The Lord never let Oliver down and as he began to develop a broken heart, his spirit became contrite. He then desired to come back and be a member of the church again. This time, he did not seek office or position. His faith was restored and so was his knowledge. He needed a broken heart and a contrite spirit to once again enjoy the full access to the transcendental world. Once this happened, David Whitmer reported that, "he died the happiest of men" (*Oliver Cowdery – Scribe, Elder, Witness,* page 351). Oliver Cowdrey's experience is a type-case of what happens to knowledge that we obtain through faith. If our faith is undermined and we begin to lose it, then the knowledge the Lord gave to us because of our faith is also lost. I have seen this happen among many who begin to lose their faith either because of sin or because they cease to nourish it. The knowledge they once possessed leaves them and they leave the faith because the knowledge that sustained it is also lost. But, Oliver Cowdrey's experience is also very helpful. The Lord never leaves us alone, and when we begin to re-establish our faith, our knowledge obtained through faith also returns.

Well, I hope this dismisses the "Mormon myth" of suggesting that once we have knowledge, we don't need faith any more. This "myth" is caused by arrogance, pride and an over-valuation of our own meager abilities when compared to those of the Lord. Indeed Isaiah was right when he wrote (Isaiah 55:8-9), *"For my thoughts are not your thoughts...saith the Lord. For as the heavens are higher than the earth, so are my ways higher than your ways, and my thoughts than your thoughts."* We can testify that we know the gospel is true for we gained this knowledge by bringing forth a broken heart and a contrite spirit; from calling ourselves unprofitable servants. And from understanding that even obedience that does not flow from these two traits, which are indeed the building blocks of faith, that even then our works, without the ratifying seal of the Holy Ghost will never be justified, meaning acceptable before the Lord. Faith is the great key, and as shown in the example of the brother of Jared's life, faith that is living and growing, drawing the Lord near to us even to the point that we can pierce the veil. **This should not be our goal however.** I will explain later why this goal, of trying to pierce the veil and have our calling and election made sure, is unwise. Indeed, having one's calling and election made sure is really up to the Lord and not up to us. To try to reverse this order is the height of arrogance, and is not prudent.

The relationship between faith, knowledge, and obedience is one where there is a progression from one event to the next, creating a non-reversible series of phenomena, known in philosophical terms as a teleology, where if one step is omitted, the next steps cannot happen. If we understand faith, knowledge, and obedience in this way, then all three principles work in harmony together to produce a great understanding of how the Lord deals with us and how we are to deal with Him. The first principle that we must understand is that of faith. Faith is not only belief, although belief is precious and an essential preliminary step. Belief carries with it a sense of innocence; children have belief in their parents, belief in their teachers and belief in simple things. As they grow older, questions come and belief is replaced with a desire for answers and empirical truth. Faith builds on belief and returns us a certitude found in coming to understand spiritual things by the power of the Holy Ghost; it comes from a broken heart and a contrite spirit and as we have learned, without these attributes, the "ends of the law" cannot be answered. This means that without faith, our obedience is much less than perfect. Faith must come first and with it, we then will have sighted obedience, not blind obedience.

With such faith and sighted obedience, we obtain knowledge from the transcendental world that produces a certitude that is unshakable. Just as Jacob testified in his encounter with the faithless Sherem, explained in Jacob 7:5, *"And he had hope to shake me from the faith, notwithstanding the many revelations and the many things which I had seen concerning these things; for I truly had seen angels, and they had ministered unto me. And also, I had heard the voice of the Lord* **speaking unto me in very word, from time to time; wherefore, I could not be shaken."**

If the Lord desires it, our vision can pierce the veil, but that will not be necessary, nor would it provide any greater certainty than that knowledge obtained transcendentally. Our goal should be to develop such faith so that piercing the veil is not necessary to obtain certitude with respect to our knowledge of the things of God. If we think that we must "see" physically before we can have that certitude, then we are sidetracked and our faith will wane. We then look beyond the mark, as it were, and our faith is no longer fed. We begin to seek extraordinary experiences and when these don't come, we try to manufacture them. What rubbish this is. We must realize that if we are sidetracked, then even the knowledge obtained by our faith can be shaken; even this knowledge can be lost. Let's seek the surer path of obtaining faith so our obedience will be sighted and then, as we feed our faith, our knowledge of God and of heavenly things will become unshakable.

With warm personal regards,

LETTER NINE

WHY FAITH MUST PRECEDE OBEDIENCE

We often have come to understand, incorrectly, that faith is a product of obedience. Faith must precede obedience so that our works can be justified. This letter will clarify why faithful obedience produces the best results. It must be clear that obedience strengthens faith it does not create it! Faith comes as a gift when we bring forth a broken heart and a contrite spirit.

Dear Missionary,

I just want to thank you so very much for your letter and the kind card for my birthday you sent last week. I appreciate also the fact that Letter Six on the relationship between grace, knowledge and justified works was one that put things into proper context for you. I was also gratified to learn of your experience learning from the Spirit. You have received an "ah-hah" as to the place you were sent on a mission and as you contemplated this inspiration, your love for the people began to grow. You said you looked forward to actually being there and could see yourself teaching the gospel to these wonderful people. That is what we call vision and it is appropriate to your circumstances. Let us move directly to your questions.

You indicated that you had heard a counselor in your branch presidency speak about part of the 130th section of the Doctrine and Covenants that we discussed in my Letter Eight. He said that the law that was irrevocably decreed in heaven was the law of obedience. In our discussions we indicated that the law that was irrevocably decreed was faith. Well, to discover the true meaning, let's look at it more closely. First, let's assume for a moment that the law is obedience. When we substitute this understanding into the scripture, it would read as follows: *"There is a law irrevocably decreed in heaven (obedience) before the foundations of this world, upon which all blessings are predicated...And when we obtain any blessing from God, it is by obedience to that law (obedience) upon which the law is predicated."* You can see from the above, that if the law were obedience, the passage would not make sense. Be obedient to the law of obedience? It can't mean this.

There is no doubt that obedience is vital, but it is **how** we are obedient that is important. The scripture states we must be obedient to that irrevocably decreed law. This is the challenge. The question naturally follows, since the scripture would not make sense if obedience were the irrevocably decreed law, what then, is this law? The first principle of the gospel is faith. We have already cited parts of the following passage from the Prophet Joseph Smith, but it bears repeating:

> Faith being the first principle in revealed religion, and the **foundation** of all righteousness, necessarily claims the first place in a course of lectures which are designed to unfold to the understanding the doctrine of Jesus Christ...Are not all your exertions of every kind, dependent on your faith? Or, may we not ask, what have you, or what do you possess, which you have not obtained by reason of your faith? Your food, your raiment, your lodgings, are they not all by reason of your faith? Reflect, and ask yourselves if these things are not so. Turn your thoughts on your own minds, and see **if faith is not the moving cause of all action** in yourselves; and, if the moving cause is you, is it not in all other intelligent beings?
>
> It is the principle by which Jehovah works, and through which he exercises power over all temporal as well as eternal things. Take this principle or attribute - for it is an attribute - from the Deity, and he would cease to exist...Had it not been for the faith which was in men, they might have spoken to the sun, the moon, the mountains, prisons, the human heart, fire, armies, the sword, or to death in vain! Faith, then, is the **first great governing principle which has power, dominion, and authority over all things; by it they exist, by it they**

are upheld, by it they are changed, or by it they remain, agreeable to the will of God. Without it there is no power, and without power there could be neither creation nor existence! (*Lectures on Faith,* Lecture 1, pages 1-5.)

What do we learn from the above quotation found in the *Lectures on Faith*? We learn that faith is the first principle of the gospel, it is the moving cause of all action, and it is a power. It holds authority over all things and that the earth and the very process of creation was accomplished by faith. If God did not have faith, He would cease to be God. If man did not have faith, all things would be vain. The scripture says (Doctrine and Covenants 8:10), *"Remember that without faith you can do nothing; therefore ask in faith. Trifle not with these things; do not ask for that which you ought not."* Thus we see that without faith, we can do absolutely nothing. Therefore, if we are obedient, without faith, nothing will happen. I have seen many cases of this. There are many Latter-day Saints who are very obedient, but have no faith. These are they that do not receive the Holy Ghost and are not justified.

Let's explore this more deeply. Paul wrote in Romans 3:20-28 the following, which I shall quote from the Revised Standard Version because it is somewhat clearer, *" For no human being will be justified in his sight by the works of the law, since through the law comes knowledge of sin. But now the righteousness of God has been manifested apart from the law, although the law and the prophets bear witness to it, the righteousness of God through faith in Jesus Christ for all who believe. For there is no distinction; since all have sinned and fall short of the glory of God, they are justified by his grace as a gift, through the redemption which is in Christ Jesus, whom God put forward as an expiation by his blood, to be received by faith... it was to prove at the present time that he himself is righteous and that he justifies him who has faith in Jesus. Then what becomes of our boasting? It is excluded. On what principle? On the principle of works? No, but on the principle of faith. For we hold that a man is justified by faith apart from works of the law."* Paul further stated in Romans 2:11-13 (King James Version), *"For there is no respect of persons with God. For as many as have sinned without law* [of faith] *shall also perish without law: and as many as have sinned in the law* [of faith] *shall be judged by the law; For not the hearers of the law are just before God, but the doers of the law* [of faith] *shall be justified."* It appears that faith is where it all begins and ends. All the works of the prophets, all of their acts were done in faith..

We are commanded to have faith; we are admonished to have our faith grow. We learned in Letter Eight that faith is a gift, given to those who bring forth a broken heart and a contrite spirit. Faith is not an "earned" blessing. We further learned that all spiritual gifts, including faith are given because of the grace of the Lord Jesus Christ; because of His compassion for us and His desire that we should come to Him for answers. These concepts were discussed in Letter Eight, but let's flesh them out further. To review, we read in 1 Corinthians 12:8-11, *"For to one is given by the Spirit the word of wisdom; to another the word of knowledge by the same Spirit; To another **faith** by the same Spirit; to another the gifts of healing by the same Spirit; To another the working of miracles; to another prophecy; to another discerning of spirits; to another divers kinds of tongues; to another the interpretation of tongues: But all these worketh that one and the selfsame Spirit, dividing to every man severally as he will."* Paul continues this thought in his letter to the Ephesians. We read in Ephesians 2:8-9, *"For by grace are ye saved through faith; and that not of yourselves: it is the gift of God: Not of works, lest any man should boast."* From these verses, we see then, that faith is a **gift of the Spirit** as is repentance and all the other gifts mentioned.

How do we obtain this gift? We certainly cannot require it of God. Gifts of the Spirit cannot be "earned" or "demanded" or "forced". Paul taught in Galatians 5:22, *"But the fruit of the Spirit is love, joy, peace, longsuffering, gentleness, goodness, **faith**."* Paul further taught that faith comes by hearing the word of God preached or taught by those who have the Spirit (Romans 10:17). Joseph Smith taught this truth exactly as Paul did. In the *Teachings of the Prophet Joseph Smith,* page 148, he taught: "Faith comes by hearing the word of God, through the TESTIMONY of the servants of God; that testimony is always attended by the Spirit." This is consistent with what the Lord taught Nicodemus as we discussed in Letter Five, as recorded in John 3. We have to be born of the Spirit to **see** the kingdom of God. Faith, as Paul taught, is a substance of things hoped for. That substance is a broken heart and a contrite spirit. Again the importance of that seminal chapter of scripture known as 2 Nephi 2 is shown to be absolutely relevant. Again, in verse 7 we read, *"Behold, he offereth himself a sacrifice for sin, to answer the ends of the law, unto all those who have a broken heart and a contrite spirit; and unto **none else can the ends of the law be answered."*** We further see that to only those who have a broken heart and a contrite spirit can the ends of the law (of faith) be answered. The Lord sacrificed Himself for such; for those who have a broken heart, as He did.

And what kind of a sacrifice does He wish in return? The law of sacrifice today is recorded in the Doctrine and Covenants 59:8, *"Thou shalt offer a sacrifice unto the Lord thy God in righteousness, even that of a broken heart and a contrite spirit."* So if we bring forth the broken heart and the contrite spirit, the Lord **gives** us faith. If we want to increase our faith we follow the pattern the Lord gave us in Luke 17:5-10 which was cited in Letter Eight. In these verses, the "take away" is that despite all of our good works, we are still unprofitable servants. We have done that which was our duty to do. With this in mind, let's look at Mosiah 4:6. *"I say unto you, if ye have come to a knowledge of the goodness of God, and his matchless power, and his wisdom, and his patience, and his long-suffering towards the children of men; and also, the atonement which has been prepared from the foundation of the world, that thereby salvation might come to him that should put his trust in the Lord, and should be diligent in keeping his commandments, and continue in the **faith** even unto the end of his life...I say, that this is the man who receiveth salvation, through the atonement which was prepared from the foundation of the world for all mankind."* Read the rest of the chapter and you will see that it is by faith that our obedience is made valid. Through the gift of faith wrought by a broken heart and a contrite spirit we become humble and receive remission of our sins. It is by faith that we perform the works of the law and by such performance is our faith made perfect. In the book of James 2:22 we read, *"Seest thou how faith wrought with his works, and by works was faith made perfect?"*

We must have faith before obedience, otherwise our obedience will not be justified; it will only lead to pride as we "pat ourselves on the back" because we will feel we had "earned" our place in the celestial kingdom. If we have faith first, then our obedience to the commandments will be justified, as Nephi told us, by the Spirit, and then our justified works will make our faith perfect. We must have faith in order to do anything. Without faith, we might be totally obedient, but such obedience runs the risk of pride, which in turn will not produce the results we desire.

To further make the point, we go to 2 Nephi 26:13, *"And that he manifesteth himself unto all those who believe in him, by the power of the Holy Ghost; yea, unto every nation, kindred, tongue, and people, working mighty miracles, signs, and wonders, among the children of men **according to their faith**."* Now let's turn to Hebrews 11:6, *"But without faith it is impossible to please him: for he that cometh to God must believe that he is, and that he is a rewarder of them that diligently seek him."* In summary then, the law irrevocably decreed in heaven is faith. We receive faith as a gift of God in direct proportion to the nature of our sacrifice, i.e. a broken heart and a contrite spirit. If these attributes are with us, then the gift of faith, which is also a power, is given unto us. President J. Reuben Clark, in his conference address of April, 1960, stated, "As I think about faith, this principle of power, I am obliged to believe that it is an intelligent force. Of what kind, I do not know. But it is superior to and overrules all other forces of which we know." (Conference Report, April 1960.) With this faith, we can then seek the grace of God found in the further gifts of repentance; we then can cleanse ourselves, ask and receive answers and, in short, bring to pass the Lord's work on the earth. Without faith, we do not please the Lord, despite our obedience. It is the obedience that comes from faith that produces the best results. When we are humble and only try to bring forth the broken heart, that in and of itself evidences faith, and the simile of planting a seed is fulfilled in this first act of faith (see Alma 32).

Let's now go back and revisit the Doctrine and Covenants verse that began this discussion, Doctrine and Covenants 130:20-21. Let's now read it like it should be read, *"There is a law, irrevocably decreed in heaven (faith) before the foundations of this world, upon which all blessings are predicated – And when we obtain any blessing from God, it is by obedience to that law (faith) upon which it is predicated."* The scripture now makes sense. We need to be obedient to the law of faith, because by faith are all things possible with God, and with faith, according to Paul (see Galatians 3:14), *"that we might receive the promise of the Spirit through faith."* Without faith we cannot please God or be justified before Him and this is the irrevocable law. Not that obedience is unnecessary, it is, but if we don't have faith, and still are obedient, such obedience is done for motives that may be less than savory like that of "earning blessings," which is not virtuous. We may then be certainly on the road that leads to pride.

Prideful obedience and seeking to "earn" blessings is surely not the meekness exhibited by disciples of God everywhere. Thus we see that even obedience performed with a wrong motive may lead us away from our Heavenly Father. Therefore, to say the first law of heaven is obedience is only half right. It is obedience to the law of faith. In Alma 32, Alma talks of developing and exercising faith. We will not go into too much depth here, however, we can say that we must have it and we must develop it to expanded heights if we are going to do the work that the Lord will have us do. Everywhere we turn in the scriptures we read of the importance of faith. It is impossible to go very far and not see the Lord's anointed exercising their faith, admonishing us to do things in faith, condemning us because we have not enough faith, telling us our faith is in the wrong place, warning us not to put our faith in our deeds, but in Christ. The list goes on and on.

Well the list may go on and on, but I must stop. I am so proud of you and your growth. To close, we may ask, is it better to obey without faith? After all, do not blessings come after the trial of our faith? The true answer to this question is found in Ether 12:6 which tells us that, you will *"receive no witness until after the trial of your faith."* There are those who say try it and then you will receive a witness of the truth of the principle you obeyed. This is true, but again in the right context. If we first have faith and then are obedient, we may indeed be tried; the witness may indeed come after a trial of our faith, but said sighted obedience then increases our faith; without it, we run a terrible risk of developing pride, which in turn kills faith. The answer then is this: be obedient, not rebellious. Rebellion comes from pride; it is a condition where we set our thoughts above God's and thereby judge our thoughts to be superior to His thoughts. We have dealt with that above. Rebellion further precludes the development of any faith whatsoever, as illustrated in this letter, by the responses of Laman and Lemuel, who said after they were obedient (but not because of their faith) in 1 Nephi 3:31, *"How is it possible that the Lord will deliver Laban into our hands? Behold, he is a mighty man, and he can command fifty, yea, even he can slay fifty; then why not us?"*

Therefore, it is better to be obedient than disobedient, but remember, be full of faith first so that your obedience will bear better fruit. Continue to bring forth the broken heart and the contrite spirit as your gifts to God and you will see that your sighted obedience will be made more perfect. It will be the Lord that will deliver to you great gifts and great success measured by Him and not by you. Truly, the Lord is bound (Doctrine and Covenants 82:10) when we do what He says **in faith**, but when we do not what he says, or even when we do what He says, without faith, we have no promise. Why? Because when we do what He says in faith, He can justify our works; without faith, the promise of justification by the Spirit, which leads to salvation and exaltation, cannot be fulfilled. The promise is not that He will give us what we want (or worse, what we think we have earned), but that He will justify us by His Spirit according to His will and our needs. As we have learned above (Galatians 3:14), we receive the promise not through deeds but by faith, which precedes the deeds. The Lord is bound indeed, meaning He is bound to justify us when we do what He says in faith, but without faith, we have no promise. I know how much the Lord loves you and I want you to know how much I love you as well. We have shared so much and will yet share many great and important things pertaining to the kingdom of the Lord. Take care of yourself and know you are in my prayers and thoughts. I care greatly about what happens to you and I hope this letter clarifies your question about the first law of heaven. It is always a pleasure to be your research assistant in His great endeavor!

With love and deep affection,

LETTER TEN

WHY PRIESTHOOD KEYS ARE VITAL

We talk about the priesthood and the need for it. We need to learn the importance of priesthood keys and how these keys are exercised. Why are there two priesthoods and what purpose is served by the Law of Moses? This knowledge will help us understand what happens when brethren participate in priesthood ordinances but are unworthy to do so.

Dear Missionary,

In other letters written to you, specifically Letter Six, Eight and Nine, we discussed relationships between some important doctrines and how these doctrines were informed by the relationship between the Father and the Son. As a missionary, understanding these relationships is pivotal in coming to know what we are to do and what we can expect God to do (see Letter Seven). In this Letter Ten, we will delve into the need for priesthood keys. These keys govern both the ordinances required to receive the Lord's gift of Atonement (including baptism) as well as direct us in how His enabling power can be used and magnified in blessing the lives of all with whom we come into contact. I think you have a preliminary understanding of such matters and are beginning to realize that without keys, which create order in the Lord's Kingdom, the ability to accept the gift of the Atonement would not be possible. For with God and His work, there is always an order to be found. We can see this in the laws of nature and science clearly, but even in transcendental matters that are found beyond the realm of empiricism, matters like faith, order is necessary. It is clear then, that in order to act in the name of the Lord, and exercise His enabling power, the keys of the priesthood are also necessary. This subject is not new to Christianity. As we survey the Christian world today, we see a range of answers to the question of who has the authority to act in the Lord's name and how is such authority given to society. Roman Catholics are clear on their authority. They follow the practice of "laying on hands" to ordain Catholic priests. For them, the pope is the successor to Peter and they claim the pope's authority over Christianity is absolute. In a like manner, Orthodox Christians look to their patriarchs, in Istanbul (formerly Constantinople), Moscow or other ethnic centers. Protestants look to educational institutions where departments of Theology confer knowledge and authority by way of a diploma to potential Protestant ministers. The laying on of hands is optional.

As you can clearly see, this matter of authority and keys is a matter of legitimacy. If purveyors of religion do not have legitimacy, their pretentions to teach us the truth are undermined. As a result, great confusion is now found among the various Christian religions of today regarding authority and the keys required to both teach and administer metaphysical truth. What I mean by metaphysical is this: how we understand the world of God and His dealings with humankind. In the days of the Savior and the original twelve apostles, legitimacy was questioned at every juncture. The Pharisees, the Sadducees, the Scribes as well as the philosophers addressed by Paul as he spoke on Mars Hill (see Acts 17:2 and 18-23), all had pretentions to legitimacy. For many of them, legitimacy was found in the "word of God" as they understood it and as they interpreted it to their followers. We will discuss how all this came to be in the letters contained in Volume II, but for now as far as the priesthood and its keys are concerned, we will confine our discussion to one regarding legitimacy. If we find claims to priesthood and priesthood keys to be illegitimate, we can properly conclude that such claims are made by a false priesthood, which does not give us the proper metaphysical understanding of God's dealings with us. Moreover, if the authority to act in God's name is illegitimate, then the doctrines that undergird such authority are also illegitimate.

When the Savior came to earth in the meridian of time, the earth lay in sin and apostasy. It was His ministry and through His apostles that He sought to remedy this condition. The Jews were in deep apostasy, which continued after His death and resurrection. At the time of the Savior, the scriptures that were most generally accepted by the Jews were fashioned into a book known as the Septuagint, completed in Alexandria, Egypt, where a large population of learned Jews lived after the times of Alexander the Great. It is a Greek translation of the Hebrew books that would make up the Old Testament and was well circulated in Palestine at the time of Jesus. The Lord would have been very familiar with this text. (It is interesting to note that the oldest New Testament texts are also written in Greek.) Between the seventh and tenth centuries A.D., Jewish scholars sought to create a Hebrew collection of the Old Testament. They met in Haifa and reviewed all the various texts produced by various Jewish traditions and produced what is called the Masoretic translation of the Old Testament texts. It was this Masoretic text (Hebrew text) that the King James translators used when translating the Old Testament into English and it was a Septuagint text (Greek text) they used for the English translation of the New Testament. This is why when you try to read verses cited from the Old Testament in the New Testament, they don't match. All of this was done in an effort to confer legitimacy on those who had lost the ability to receive revelation. Because the ancient Jewish and Christian worlds knew they no longer received revelation, they looked to these texts, to those who indeed did receive revelation, to fortify their own legitimacy. Hence, in the Protestant churches, which found both authority and legitimacy solely in the texts of the Bible, to the priesthood of the Catholic and Orthodox branches of Christianity, which sought confirmation of their legitimacy and authority through these ancient texts.

This of course creates a dilemma. What is legitimate authority and what constitutes the ability to act in the name of God? Moreover, the ability to sort these questions out with respect to legitimacy also then will define the correct metaphysics, a correct understanding of God's world and how He deals with humankind.

Hugh Nibley, in a commencement address given at Brigham Young University, August 19, 1993 clarifies more closely this dilemma:

> Twenty years ago on this same occasion, I gave the opening prayer, in which I said: "We are met here today clothed in the black robes of a false priesthood." Many have asked me since whether I actually said such a shocking thing, but nobody has ever asked what I meant by it....Why a priesthood? Because these robes originally denoted those who had taken clerical orders, and a college was a "mystery" with all the rites, secrets, oaths, degrees, tests, feasts, and solemnities that go with initiation to higher knowledge.
>
> But why false? Because it is borrowed finery, coming down to us through a long line of unauthorized imitators. It was not until 1893 that "an intercollegiate commission was formed to draft a uniform code for caps, gowns, and hoods" in the United States. Before that there were no rules – you designed your own; and that liberty goes as far back as these fixings can be traced. The late Roman emperors...marked each step in the decline of their power and glory by the addition of some new ornament to the resplendent vestments that proclaimed their sacred office and dominion. ("Leaders and Managers," page 1.)

Dr. Nibley then points out that these attempts to legitimate such metaphysical authority actually came from the vestments of the true priesthood, the priesthood introduced to the House of Israel by Moses and continued for centuries in the temple at Jerusalem. These were of course the ordinances and vestments given by the Lord not only to Moses, but originally to Adam, Enoch, Noah, and Abraham. "There is another type of robe and headdress described in Exodus and Leviticus and the third book of Josephus' *Antiquities,* i.e., the white robe and linen cap of the Hebrew priesthood...They were given up entirely, however, with the passing of the temple and were never even imitated again by the Jews." ("Leaders and Managers," page 1.) It is interesting to note that these vestments of a false priesthood became more ornate and colorful even as such metaphysical pretention to authority and its keys declined. It is also true from what Dr. Nibley has told us that legitimate metaphysical authority and its keys were contained in the Hebrew priesthood and its ordinances. As the true metaphysical authority passed away in apostasy, Dr. Nibley continues:

> Both the black and white robes proclaim a primary concern for the things of the mind and the spirit, sobriety of life, and concentration of purposes removed from the largely mindless, mechanical routines of your everyday world. Cap and gown announced that the wearer had accepted certain rules of living and been tested in special kinds of knowledge. ("Leaders and Managers," page 3.)

It is clear that the Lord intended the authority of His priesthood to convey special knowledge upon its recipients. The keys to this special knowledge were given anciently to those who performed ordinances in the temple. Likewise, the keys of His priesthood would be given in temples. This was the case in 1836 when they were given to Joseph Smith and Oliver Cowdery in Kirtland, Ohio, and when they were given to Peter, James, and John on the Mount of Transfiguration. Mountains are always a "type" of temple and are used in lieu of temples when they are not available. This can happen either when they are physically not present or when they have become devoid of the Lord's Spirit, as was the case in the meridian of time. Priesthood keys and temples are inseparably linked together as the scriptures clearly demonstrate. The way we receive the priesthood is through ordination by one who has the authority and permission to perform the ordination. We read in Luke 9:1, *"Then he called his twelve disciples together, and gave them power and authority over all devils, and to cure diseases."* This was done by ordination, as seen in John 15:16, *"Ye have not chosen me, but I have chosen you, and ordained you."* From the Webster's dictionary, we read the following definition of the word *ordain*: "to invest officially (as by the laying on of hands) with ministerial or priestly authority."

Jesus laid his hands on the heads of the apostles and invested them with ministerial and priestly authority. Thus all of the apostles were invested with the Savior's authority to not only be able to rebuke devils and disease, but to administer in the affairs of His church. Now we come to the question of priesthood keys. The Roman

Catholics believe that it was Peter alone who received the keys while Protestants believe Peter received the keys as a "trustee" of sorts for everyone in the community of Christ (known as the body of Christ). Authority was not conferred upon the original twelve apostles by a university degree, nor was it given to them because they had taken classes and distinguished themselves academically. It was given to them by ordination as the Savior, for reasons known only to Him, had called them and ordained them personally. Their calling did not occur because they had distinguished themselves in a worldly sense, but because they were foreordained in our pre-mortal life to these positions. Once ordained, they were then in a position to receive the special knowledge promised in such an ordination.

We read of the apostles receiving the keys of the priesthood in Matthew 17 when the Lord took Peter, James, and John upon the Mount of Transfiguration. Before we discuss the full importance of the keys of the priesthood, let us unpack your questions by taking the first part regarding Peter, James and John. You asked me about them, when they formed the First Presidency, and when this was done, shouldn't there have been three apostles named to the Quorum of the Twelve? The answer is yes. We know from the New Testament that other members of the Quorum of the Twelve were added to that governing body. We read in the book of Acts of others that were called, including in Acts 9, the calling of Paul. We know of at least three additional members that were added to the Twelve. Although matters of church organization and procedure have always been subject to change, the apostolic succession is bedrock doctrine and it was established in the New Testament. This succession is fundamental and is carried forward in the exact same manner today as when it was established and documented in the New Testament.

With these keys, the powers of knowledge, even special knowledge, as well as the powers of heaven could be unlocked to bless the lives of all men and women by bringing them the ordinances of exaltation. This special knowledge is contained in the ordinances of the Melchizedek priesthood as we read in Doctrine and Covenants 84:19-21, *"And this greater priesthood administereth the gospel and holdeth the key of the mysteries of the kingdom, even the key of the knowledge of God. Therefore, in the ordinances thereof, the power of godliness is manifest. And without the ordinances thereof, and the authority of the priesthood, the power of godliness is not manifest unto men in the flesh."* We are not talking about those who later became Gnostics; those who subscribe to the doctrine of "special knowledge" reserved for only a few enlightened people. No, this special knowledge is for all who receive the ordinances of the Melchizedek priesthood.

This is a critical concept for you to understand; that the apostles at the meridian of time were empowered by the authority of the Lord in like manner. Such authority was given to apostles then and now through the proper exercise of priesthood keys, to do exactly the same things today that were done then. All missionaries, both brothers and sisters, have likewise been empowered with this same authority by those who currently exercise the keys of the priesthood. This priesthood was designed from the meridian of time to be ever present so that the keys could be used to bless the lives of all who embraced the gift of the Atonement. We read in Acts 1 about the process of calling a new member to the Twelve. We therefore know of at least three added and mentioned in the New Testament. As we examine this more closely, we note that the first addition to the Quorum of the Twelve was Matthias. We read about him in Acts 1:22-26. From these verses, it was clear that Matthias replaced Judas in the quorum and that the first presidency had not yet been organized. You will note that Matthias was "numbered with the eleven apostles," meaning that there were only twelve. These verses show that the Quorum of Twelve Apostles was the governing body of the church. It is so with us today, if the president of the church dies, the First Presidency is dissolved and the Quorum of the Twelve runs the church. Thus, we can show that it is the Quorum of the Twelve that is always with us in the true church and never is dissolved unless the church has fallen completely into apostasy.

The office of President of the Quorum of the Twelve is also firmly established. Upon Peter were the keys of the kingdom confirmed (Matthew 16:16-19). They were subsequently conferred upon all of the Twelve (see Matthew 18:18). So, it is clear that all of the Twelve had the keys, not just Peter. All of the apostles had the authority and they all held the keys; however, Peter was specifically called by the Lord to exercise these keys and as long as Peter lived, he would do so. If Peter were taken in death, then the next senior apostle would have been in a position to exercise all the keys. As such, he would be able to use these keys as the Lord directed the work through him.

The seniority among the Twelve was clearly established in Luke 6:13-16, Mark 3:13-21 and Matthew 10:2-4. Why does this seem so important to New Testament writers? It is because the senior apostle is the man in whom all keys to the priesthood are vested. The ancients knew this and were focused on letting us know this as well. In fact, the primacy of Peter, according to his seniority is absolute for the Catholic faith; if there was no seniority, the claim of the Roman Church to build it's organization on Peter would be specious at best and would underscore Protestant claims to authority at worst. So, in these three scriptural accounts, it seems that while many of the verses are the same, others listed are different. However, in all accounts, they begin with Peter, the most senior apostle. Elder Bruce R. McConkie gives us the harmonized list:

> From the accounts of the three synoptists, it is apparent that members of the original Twelve were: Simon Peter, James (son of Zebedee), John (his brother), Andrew (Peter's brother), Philip, Bartholomew (or Nathanael), Matthew (also called Levi), Thomas (or Didymus), James (son of Alpheus), Judas (also known s Labbeus or Thaddeus), Simon Zelotes (called also Sinon the Canaanite), and Judas Iscariot. Brief biographical comments about each are found in *Jesus the Christ*, by Elder James E. Talmage, pp. 218-226.
>
> As vacancies occurred in this Twelve and in the one organized among the Nephites, other worthy brethren were selected to replace the missing apostles. Apostasy on both hemispheres brought an end to authoritative apostolic administration as given by Jesus. Indeed, the presence or absence of true apostles in any church is conclusive proof of the divinity or falsity of that ecclesiastical organization. (*Doctrinal New Testament Commentary*, Volume I, page 211.)

What all this means is that there were more than twelve apostles, even in the days of the Savior, but only one Quorum of the Twelve. These biblical verses further tell us that the Quorum was not a static group, even though it was subject to an order of seniority, but one in which new members would be called as vacancies occurred. This also shows that seniority is vital in being able to exercise the keys given to all of the Twelve, Peter being first to exercise these keys. But the fact remains that all had the keys (see Matthew 18:18), hence, the order of how these keys were to be used is also clearly established.

Now let us consider more closely the keys of the priesthood these apostles held. It is significant that in Mark 17, when Jesus points out that Peter, James and John were called first, He is really confirming to us that these three were with Him on the Mount of Transfiguration, received the keys of the priesthood and, by being so ordered when discussing the Twelve, shows that they were the original First Presidency of the church. We know that Peter was the President of this Quorum of the Twelve Apostles because he was the senior apostle named in all the accounts shown above. But also because the Lord had specifically called him out from the other members of the Twelve in Matthew 16, and had promised him the keys of the kingdom. So why did the Savior in the gospel of Mark call out Peter, James, and John and call them Boanerges, or Sons of Thunder? It was partly because of the intensity of their character, but also because they were the other original brethren called to the First Presidency.

So, what do we know so far? We know that there was a Quorum of Twelve Apostles that was to be continuous. As former members either apostatized or were killed, new members were added to it. We know that the keys of the kingdom were given to all members of it, but that the President of the Twelve, established by seniority, could exercise those keys. We do not know exactly when the First Presidency was organized, but it was clear that it was organized before the Savior's mission was concluded. We see (in Matthew 17) that the Lord took Peter, James and John up on the Mount of Transfiguration with Him. It was there they received the keys of Moses, Elijah and Elias. These are the keys of the gathering of

Israel, the sealing power, and the keys to eternal marriage or, the Abrahamic Covenant. In a like manner, in this dispensation, the senior apostles, Joseph Smith and Oliver Cowdery, the two men who were actually ordained by Peter, James and John, and therefore were, like them, the senior apostles on earth at this time. It was to Peter, James and John these senior apostles to whom the keys were given at the time of the Savior, and it was to these two senior brethren, in a like manner as in previous times to whom the keys of the priesthood were restored as well (see Doctrine and Covenants section 110).

We further know, with respect to the members of the Quorum of the Twelve Apostles that all of them held all of the keys of the kingdom, which were sealed upon them at the time of their ordination. These keys do not become active until an apostle becomes the senior apostle, not by age but by ordination seniority. That means that when the senior apostle dies, the next apostle in seniority of ordination, not of age, is now able to exercise all of the keys. It will always be thus, that when the senior apostle dies, the remaining members of the Twelve meet. They do not vote on who should become the president of the church because the new senior apostle is now able to exercise all of the keys; just as it was with Peter when the Savior was no longer personally present upon the earth. As such, all of his keys become active and vested in him and he becomes the President of the Church. It is not true that each of the Twelve have just one or some of the keys. They all have all of them and these keys were given to them at the time of their ordination to the Twelve. However, they are not authorized to exercise these keys without permission until they become the senior apostle. There can be more than twelve men who are members of the Quorum of the Twelve, just as it appeared to be so in the early days of the church discussed above. Today, there are fifteen men who have been ordained apostles and have been set apart as members of the Quorum of the Twelve.

Now you can see that more than twelve men are members of the Quorum of the Twelve. Because of this, in Jerusalem at the time of Christ and in America there were twelve men in each place that were all members of the Quorum of the Twelve. Were they ordered in seniority from one to twenty four? Yes. Those of the Twelve who were in America were called the twelve Disciples and although they were apostles in every sense, they were responsible to the Twelve in Jerusalem. In 1 Nephi 12:8-10 we read, *"And the angel spake unto me, saying: Behold the twelve disciples of the Lamb, who are chosen to minister unto thy seed. And he said unto me: Thou rememberest the twelve apostles of the Lamb? Behold they are they who shall judge the twelve tribes of Israel; wherefore, the twelve ministers of thy seed shall be judged of them; for ye are of the house of Israel. And these twelve ministers whom thou beholdest shall judge thy seed..."* President Joseph Fielding Smith wrote:

> While in every instance the Nephite Twelve are spoken of as disciples, the fact remains that they had been endowed with divine authority to be special witnesses for Christ among their own people. Therefore, they were virtually apostles to the Nephite race, although their jurisdiction was, as revealed to Nephi, eventually to be subject to the authority and jurisdiction of Peter and the Twelve chosen in Palestine. (*Doctrines of Salvation*, Vol. III, page 158.)

All of this is so because the kingdom of God is a house of order, just as you would suppose. It is not a place where there exists diverse and contradictory doctrine like what we find in Protestant churches today, each claiming authority over each other's flocks. While this is going on, the Catholic priesthood is claiming authority over Protestant flocks and quite frankly, the Catholics have a superior claim to authority. Protestant churches are extremely weak when it comes to tracing their authority and it shows in the number of denominations of Protestantism that exist today. So we see, my friend, that there is order in the kingdom of God. That order is shown in the seniority that exists among the Twelve. This seniority exists among all the apostles who belong to the Quorum of the Twelve, irrespective of how many actual members there are. The senior Nephite disciple, while exercising the keys for the Nephites, is still subject to the authority of the Twelve in Jerusalem and in the spirit world, where the two churches come together. Peter, the senior apostle, presides over all of them (see Mormon 3:18-19).

Moreover, we read in the book of Acts of other apostles, for example, Paul. We do not read of his ordination, but we know he was an apostle because he tells us so on numerous occasions. We now have at least 14 men who were ordained apostles, and set apart as members of the Quorum of the Twelve, but are there others? Yes, Barnabas was considered an apostle, although not a member of the Twelve (see Acts 14:14). So it seems that after the First Presidency was organized, new apostles were called as others were killed (as in the case of James - see Acts 12:2). This is the order of the church with respect to this Quorum. There were always to be apostles among us (see Ephesians 4) as long as the church was valid. We have carefully chronicled the continuous apostasy and the Great Apostasy in the letters found in Volume II. History has validated the occurrence of inevitable apostasy and when it becomes rampant, the Lord took the priesthood and its keys away from the earth. With the loss of the Twelve and the First Presidency, there was no authority left on earth. Even those who had priesthood authority did not have the keys necessary to ordain others. This fact is the consummate tragedy of contention and apostasy, and we are seeing a similar pattern emerging today. The above should answer questions you have about the keys of the priesthood, why they are so important and why they reside today with the leadership of the Church of Jesus Christ of Latter-day Saints.

The letters found in Volume II will demonstrate the history of how these keys came to be on the earth at the time of Christ. The Old Testament gives accounts of him who held the sealing power, Elijah; of him who held the keys of the gathering of Israel, Moses; and of him who held the keys of priesthood, Elias (meaning messenger). From the New Testament account, this Elias was identified as John the Baptist and so did not this same Elias, who gave priesthood keys to Peter, James, and John on that very Mount of Transfiguration, also visit Joseph Smith and Oliver Cowdery as recorded in section 13 of the Doctrine and Covenants? And from section 110 of the Doctrine and Covenants we learn of others who were also called Elias that came to Joseph and Oliver and undoubtedly visited Peter, James, and

John as well. It is clear that those who held the keys in former times came to Peter, James, and John at the meridian of time to restore them again to the earth. The Lord knew that a Great Apostasy would occur and his prophets and apostles declared its beginning at the meridian of time. It is therefore the pattern of the Lord to restore the keys of the priesthood in the same manner in the latter-days as He did in meridian times.

We declare forcefully that this event, the "restitution of all things" spoken of by Peter, has occurred! In our day, apostasy continues, but rarely do we read or hear from these who leave the fold that they have received either the priesthood from those who held it at the time of the Savior when we know it was upon the earth, or that they have received keys in the same manner as they were given in former times. For them, this is a big problem. The pattern for restoration is set and is clear; it has been faithfully documented in the Bible and such documentation stands as a witness for today. All who claim authority from God and the ability to exercise such authority must follow the pattern established by the Savior in the meridian of time as faithfully outlined in the Bible. There have been many omissions to this volume of scripture, but with respect to these matters, the Bible has faithfully reported both the events of the original establishment of the priesthood along with its attendant keys and has authentically chronicled the events that must come to restore such priesthood and its necessary keys.

Now, you asked a related question concerning priesthood authority and the ability to pass it on if it is done by an inactive or less worthy member. What about his priesthood? Is such an ordination under these circumstances still legitimate or when is it no longer valid? The answer to this question is yes, the ordination is still valid. There is a caveat to it being legitimate however. Someone who holds the priesthood keys must sanction such an ordination. If such a sanction is not given, then any ordination, even by worthy priesthood bearers, is no longer valid. So the complete answer is this: when those who hold the keys approve such an ordination, it is valid. If unworthy priesthood bearers continue in unworthiness, such a man's priesthood lapses. This is the time when the priesthood a man holds can become invalid. It is interesting to note here that if a man has been ordained to the Melchizedek priesthood and his life becomes unworthy and he dies, then when we do the temple work for such an individual, as part of that work he is ordained again to that priesthood showing that the previous ordination was no longer valid due to his inactivity or unworthiness. Let us begin our analysis with some verses that usually cause some confusion with respect to this. We read in Doctrine and Covenants 121:36-37, *"That the rights of the priesthood are inseparably connected with the powers of heaven, and that the powers of heaven cannot be controlled nor handled only upon the principles of righteousness. That they may be conferred upon us, it is true; but when we undertake to cover our sins, or to gratify our pride, our vain ambition, or to exercise control or dominion or compulsion upon the souls of the children of men, in any degree of unrighteousness, behold, the heavens withdraw themselves; the Spirit of the Lord is grieved; and when it is withdrawn, Amen to the priesthood or the authority of that man."*

This scripture sets out the general parameters of when priesthood authority is no longer valid. This means that when the Spirit is grieved, and when such a person does not move to restore it, the priesthood of such a man is invalid but not illegitimate. In other words, such a man no longer seeks to repent to become justified by the Spirit. The priesthood for that man, shall we say, goes dormant; it is no longer able to bless his life. However, with respect to those who receive ordinances, like the sacrament, at his hands, those who receive such ordinances, for them the ordinance is still legitimate and valid. Why? First of all, the assignment to perform ordinances comes from those who hold the keys and the Lord honors them and sustains them in that decision. Second, those who receive ordinances from those that are not worthy to perform them have trusted those who hold the keys and therefore they have no knowledge of the unworthiness of the man performing the ordinance. The unworthy priesthood holder will be held accountable before God; this is a position in which I would NOT like to find myself. I must remind you here however, that being worthy does not mean being perfect! It does mean that we are justified (by the Holy Ghost) in performing such an ordinance. As we discussed in Letter Six, the letter dealing with justification, all ordinances of the priesthood must be sealed by the Holy Spirit of Promise (Doctrine and Covenants 132:7) for them to be valid. All right, so far so good.

But what if this man is asked to perform an ordinance such as ordaining another to the priesthood? Will the ordination of the second person be valid? The answer to this question is, yes; the ordination is still valid again if sanctioned by those who hold the keys. This is a good time to explain how the power of God is given to man and how the keys of the priesthood are inseparably connected to the powers of heaven. As we began our discussion about the priesthood, I cited above Doctrine and Covenants 121:36-37. We learned from these verses that the priesthood could be conferred upon us, but unless the priesthood was handled with righteousness not seeking to compel obedience, but seeking after the welfare of mankind through gentle persuasion, the preceding verses are now relevant. Continuing in section 121:34-35 we read, *"Behold, there are many called, but few are chosen. And why are they not chosen? Because their hearts are set so much upon the things of this world, and aspire to the honors of men, that they do not learn this one lesson."* What is that lesson, well we now go back to verse 36, *"That the rights of the priesthood are inseparably connected to the powers of heaven..."* This nexus between the powers of heaven and the condition of our hearts is vital when we speak about the priesthood and the validity or legitimacy of any ordination to the priesthood.

There is a scriptural example that seems to be right on point here. It comes from Mosiah in the Book of Mormon. In Mosiah 9, we begin to read of the account of Zeniff and his people. We learn that he was a righteous man and held keys. Why? Because at the end of his life, we see that he conferred his kingdom on his son. In Mosiah 10:22 we read, *"And now I, being old, did confer the kingdom upon one of my sons; therefore, I say no more..."* He conferred a kingdom, meaning he had keys to confer upon one of his sons who happened to be called, Noah. This new king Noah did not honor his priesthood, nor did he follow the gospel plan of his father. He in fact released all of the priests his father had consecrated (see Mosiah 11:5) and replaced them with ones more in line with his wickedness. We must assume that the priesthood was conferred upon Noah, since he became the king after his father's death, and that he, Noah, was at one time righteous. Well, he didn't remain righteous and began to be wicked. Our first reaction with respect to these new priests is that their ordination was not valid. King Noah was a wicked man by the time he did this and therefore, we mistakenly assume that since these new priests were wicked, the transfer of the priesthood was not valid. Most of them were indeed wicked, but not all of them. One of these new priests was a man named Alma and when Abinadi came to preach, Alma believed the words of Abinadi.

It is interesting that Abinadi recognized the authority of the wicked priests as valid when he stated in Mosiah 12:25-27, *"And now Abinadi said unto them: Are you priests, and pretend to teach this people, and to understand the spirit of prophesying, and yet desire to know of me what these things mean? I say unto you, wo be unto you for perverting the ways of the Lord! For if ye understand these things ye have not taught them; therefore, ye have perverted the ways of the Lord. Ye have not applied your hearts to understanding; therefore, ye have not been wise..."* We see here that Abinadi recognized that their ordination was legitimate, and yet they were not faithful to their ordination because of their behavior. Moreover, because of this, the ordination was to their condemnation. They would be held to account for having received the priesthood and not living worthy to exercise it. We know the rendering of this verse is correct because Alma did repent when he listened to the words of Abinadi. We read in Mosiah 23:9 his words, *"But remember the iniquity of king Noah and his priests; and I myself was caught in a snare, and did many things which were abominable in the sight of the Lord, which caused me sore repentance."*

Why was Abinadi able to preach so forcefully to King Noah and his priests? It is because he too was filled with meekness, faith, and charity towards them. He was not arrogant; he loved them enough to accept this mission call. He went because he loved the Lord and because he loved them in the same manner that the Lord did. He gave perfect evidence of that love as he gave his life in witnessing to them (and subsequently to the world through the Book of Mormon), that his testimony was true. It was so powerful that even though only Alma and a few others were converted, it sealed up those that did not heed this witness eternally to God; they will have no excuse. But more pertinent, look at the work Alma did and look at the harvest of souls that occurred because of Abinadi's witness. It is indeed miraculous.

Because of Abinadi's witness, Alma repented of his evil doings. When Alma became converted and sought the Spirit of the Lord, he went with others who also repented (see Mosiah 18) to the Waters of Mormon. As he was now in a position to be justified by the Spirit, he did not need to be re-ordained even though a priesthood holder who was unworthy originally ordained him. And this ordination was still deemed valid even though he too was living unworthily after the ordination. Alma's original ordination was legitimate because he had received his priesthood through the proper use of the keys of the priesthood given to Zeniff and then to Noah. When he heard the message of the prophets, he repented. He was the only priest of Noah that did repent, and because he did, he was able to baptize (because he had the authority to do so) those who had come with him to the Waters of Mormon.

So, what do we learn from this? We now understand two things. First, we learn that it takes powerful witnesses clothed in meekness and in faith to bring about great conversion. Second, we learn that even if a priesthood holder goes inactive, his priesthood as far as he is concerned is dormant. This was certainly true of Alma. If he is to perform any function with respect to the dormant priesthood he holds, someone who holds the keys of the priesthood must allow him to do so through an authorizing act. If no such enabling authority is present, and the Holy Spirit of Promise does not seal actions performed by such a priesthood holder, such ordinations or other actions undertaken by his unauthorized use of the priesthood are invalid and void. What about ordinances in which he has participated when he was worthy? If he repents, as Alma did, the Spirit re-enters his life and then the ordinances that were performed on his behalf like marriage and temple blessings are also restored. If he remains in an unworthy state, then these blessings conferred upon him when he was worthy are no longer valid as well. Why? It is because the seal of justification, the seal of the Holy Spirit of Promise is broken and when this happens, the ordinance is no longer valid. The key for Alma, and for that matter for all of us is the gift of repentance so that we can access these blessings for our lives. It is verily true that the blessings of heaven are inseparably connected to the powers of heaven and the realization of these priesthood blessings, as we discovered in the Doctrine and Covenants verses cited above, comes because our heart is right before God,

This nexus between a right heart and power in the priesthood comes back again to the prerequisite of being able to receive all blessings and that prerequisite is faith. Pride, arrogance and having our hearts set on the things of this world, such as aspiring to the honors of men, are exactly the conditions of the heart that are repugnant to the powers of heaven. They are repugnant to the justifying influence of the Holy Ghost. We have learned in the previous letters already that faith is a gift conditioned upon a broken heart and a contrite spirit. This, along with meekness, are particularly relevant conditions to the Melchizedek priesthood. Since we have used an example from the Book of Mormon to illustrate how keys work, it is important to understand that the priesthood involved was the Melchizedek priesthood. The priesthood of the Book of Mormon was Melchizedek and here is why. The Nephite priesthood and the exercise of this priesthood comes about under the direction of those who hold the keys in the New World. Why is this so? We will find that the Nephite priesthood is not the Aaronic or Levitical priesthood of the Old Testament, but is in fact the Melchizedek priesthood that has always been upon the earth, but just not widely available to the House of Israel. We will find that in the New World, the priesthood works exactly like it does in the Old World. Lehi was a descendant of Joseph (1 Nephi 5:14) meaning he had a right to the Melchizedek priesthood (see Genesis 49:25-26). We read in 1 Nephi 1:8-13 of Lehi's vision. We learn here that he was called to lead his family out of Jerusalem to the promised land described by Moses in Genesis 49:25. This was to be the land reserved for Joseph and therefore, the priesthood with which he was empowered to claim the land for the descendants of Joseph was the Melchizedek priesthood.

Thus the priesthood held by the Nephites was the Melchizedek priesthood and not Aaronic priesthood and it was by the Melchizedek priesthood by which they performed their ordinances. And as we have shown, the descendants of Lehi were of Joseph and not descendants of Levi (he to whom the Aaronic priesthood was promised), we concluded above that the authority they used had to be Melchizedek, given to Lehi by God himself, just as the Prophet Joseph Smith taught. And since we know that the Book of Mormon, contains "the fullness of the everlasting gospel," it must needs be preached and administered under the authority of the Melchizedek priesthood. We learn early on that Lehi is a descendant of Joseph through Manasseh; but according to Elder Erastus Snow:

> The prophet Joseph informed us that the record of Lehi was contained in the first 116 pages that were first translated and then stolen, and of which an abridgement was made in the First Book of Nephi; Lehi was of Manasseh, but Ishmael was of the lineage of Ephraim…his sons married into Lehi's family and Lehi's sons married Ishmael's daughters, thus fulfilling the words of Jacob upon Ephraim and Manasseh recorded in Genesis 48. (*Journal of Discourses,* vol. 23, pages 184-185.)

It is in Genesis 48 that we learn of Jacob adopting Ephraim and Manasseh as his own children with Ephraim being put before Manasseh, by saying in verse 19, *"but truly his younger brother shall be greater than he, and his seed shall become a multitude of nations."* The Melchizedek priesthood was to be part of Joseph's inheritance. Ephraim and Manasseh are birthright sons of Joseph, but Ephraim will hold the keys. This is why most all who receive a Patriarchal Blessing are declared from the tribe of Ephraim, as they are to be gathered first. Then through this priesthood, which belongs to Ephraim by birthright, the other tribes will be gathered. Now, when the families of Lehi, from Manasseh, and Ishmael, from Ephraim, intermarried, the promise made to Joseph made through his father, Israel, was fulfilled. Joseph was united together and their descendants then were able to produce the record of Joseph, which includes both Ephraim and Manasseh. Their record would be put together with the record of Judah, as prophesied by Ezekiel in chapter 36 of his record and be sent forth to all the ends of the earth. Has this not happened?

This is important because in Genesis 49, we read that Jacob (Israel) gave his son Joseph a blessing. In it he promised Joseph in verses 22, and 25-26, *"Joseph is a fruitful bough, even a fruitful bough by a well; whose branches run over the wall...Even by the God of thy father, who shall help thee; and by the Almighty, who shall bless thee with blessings of heaven above, blessings of the deep that lieth under, blessings of the breasts, and of the womb: The blessings of thy father have prevailed above the blessings of my progenitors unto the utmost bound of the everlasting hills: they shall be on the head of Joseph..."* Joseph would indeed become a mighty people gathered from all nations to enjoy the blessings of eternal increase (seed or posterity) that have prevailed over all the progenitors of Israel. The land given to Joseph's descendants is to be a land given by covenant, even to the everlasting hills. Read your patriarchal blessing and see if the blessings of Abraham, Isaac, and Jacob were not also promised to you? If they were, look at your lineage; if you are of Ephraim or Manasseh, as most are, you have received the gospel as part of the fulfillment of the covenant blessings promised to Joseph through these brothers as heirs of the promise the Lord made to them when Israel (Jacob) adopted them.

The above account of the priesthood promised to Joseph is important. Why? It is because of what will now be explained, the fact that the priesthood is divided into different spheres for different purposes. Let us remember that the priesthood originally given to Adam was the Melchizedek priesthood. This priesthood was patriarchal and extended from Adam through Enoch and Noah to Abraham. We read in Abraham 1:2-3 about this priesthood, *"And, finding there was greater happiness and peace and rest for me, I sought for the blessings of the fathers, and the right whereunto I should be ordained to administer the same; having been myself a follower of righteousness, desiring also to be one who possessed great knowledge, and to be a greater follower of righteousness, and to possess a greater knowledge, and to be a father of many nations, a prince of peace, and desiring to receive instructions, and to keep the commandments of God, I became a rightful heir, a High Priest, holding the right belonging to the fathers. It was conferred upon me from the fathers; it came down from the fathers, from the beginning of time..."* Here we see that the only priesthood that was on the earth was the Melchizedek priesthood from the times of Adam down to Abraham.

The Aaronic priesthood or Levitical priesthood was introduced to us as part of the Law of Moses as a preparatory priesthood given to man because in the days of Moses, their hearts were not right and they were set upon the honors and glories of men found in the telestial world. How was this priesthood, the Aaronic or Levitical priesthood to work? First, we know from the Old Testament, that the tribe of Levi was to bear the priesthood and perform the ordinances according to the Law of Moses, but this priesthood was the Aaronic or, as explained in the Old Testament, it was also called the Levitical priesthood (see Ezekiel 44:15). In chapter 18 of the Book of Numbers, we read that the Levites did not receive a land inheritance in Caanan, but instead were consecrated to the Lord as a substitute for the firstborn not taken during the plagues in Egypt (see Numbers 8:14-16). They were to assist the priests at the temple and perform the temple ordinances given through the Law of Moses. We further know from Paul that this Aaronic or Levitical priesthood was not sufficient to produce exaltation. In Hebrews 7:11 Paul explains, *"If therefore perfection were by the Levitical priesthood, (for under it the people received the law,) what further need was there that another priest should rise after the order of Melchisedec, and not be called after the order of Aaron?"* We learn from this that the priesthood held by the Jews, given to them by Moses, was insufficient to produce a fullness of the gospel.

The Levitical or Aaronic priesthood was a preparatory priesthood and the associated Law of Moses was to be fulfilled in the due time of the Lord. The New Testament is filled and replete with references to that effect. The Savior told His disciples and the world that the Law of Moses was fulfilled in Him. In His ministry, He declared early on in Luke 4:18-19, *"The Spirit of the Lord is upon me, because he hath anointed me to preach the gospel to the poor; he hath sent me to heal the brokenhearted, to preach deliverance to the captives, and recovering of sight to the blind, to set at liberty them that are bruised, To preach the acceptable year of the Lord."* And again in the Sermon on the Mount, He said, *"Think not that I am come to destroy the law, or the prophets: I am not come to destroy, but to fulfill."* (Matthew 5:17.) The Law of Moses is fulfilled in the coming of the Lord; all of the thousands of acts that were to be performed under the Law of Moses were fulfilled in the coming of the Son of Man. Peter tells us that we are not exalted by the Law of Moses when he told the early members of the church at Jerusalem in Acts 15:8-11, *"And God, which knoweth the hearts, bare them witness, giving them the Holy Ghost, even as he did unto us; And put no difference between us and them, purifying their hearts by **faith**. Now therefore why tempt ye God, to put a yoke upon the neck of the disciples, which neither our fathers nor we were able to bear? But we believe that through the grace of the Lord Jesus Christ we shall be saved, even as they."* Peter is telling us that the Law of Moses could be characterized as divine command theory, given at Sinai to the children of Israel because not only were their hearts set upon wealth and the honors of men, they could not embrace the humble gift they needed to offer to God, the gift of a broken heart and a contrite spirit. The love of God had "waxed cold" in their hearts and they needed this divine command theory to correct this hard-hearted condition. The Law of Moses was a taskmaster just as Paul suggested above; love was not the motivator, but fear of retribution. The Law of Moses was given to the House of Israel as an act of love so that they would not be destroyed at Sinai, as we shall see.

After the Savior's earthly mission was complete, while on the road to Emmaus, He told Luke and Cleopas in Luke 24:44, *"And he said unto them, These are the words which I spake unto you, while I was yet with you, that all things must be fulfilled, which were written in the law of Moses, and in the prophets, and in the psalms, concerning me."* Paul understood this fact; the Law of Moses was insufficient to produce salvation and he so declared in Galatians 3:24, *"Wherefore the law was our schoolmaster to bring us unto Christ, that we might be justified by faith."* And of course the Book of Mormon teaches us this principle with perfection. In 3 Nephi 15:2-5, the Lord Himself declared to us the following, *"And it came to pass that when Jesus had said these words he perceived that there were some among them who marveled, and wondered what he would concerning the law of Moses; for they understood not the saying that old things had passed away, and that all things had become new. And he said unto them: Marvel not that I said unto you that old things had passed away, and that all things had become new. Behold, I say unto you that the law is fulfilled that was given unto Moses. Behold, I am he that gave the law, and I am he who covenanted with my people Israel; therefore, the law in me is fulfilled, for I have come to fulfil the law; therefore it hath an end."*

Why is the Law of Moses fulfilled in Christ and do we really accept the fact that it is? We have all come in some measure to follow the Lord based on the divine command theory. It is hard in this world not to be tainted by it and so, unfortunately, we seek to justify ourselves by the law, by obedience to the law instead of looking to the gift of the Atonement and its attendant healing provided by the Holy Ghost through justification and sanctification. This is why Peter said, as quoted above, that neither their fathers nor they were able to completely conform in every detail to the Law of Moses. This is why Peter identified the law as a yoke. He knew that it was impossible to gain salvation under this yoke but that we would be trained by it to accept the yoke of Christ. The Savior stated clearly (Matthew 11:29-30), *"Take my yoke upon you, and learn of me; for I am meek and lowly in heart: and ye shall find rest unto your souls. For my yoke is easy, and my burden is light."* The Lord never said we need not be obedient, but we need to be obedient in faith and virtue, not to avoid punishments or gain rewards. His yoke is easy because **HE is the reward!**

We see this in the way He came to earth. He was the creator, the mighty Jehovah, second member of the Godhead, yet He gave up this power, left it with His Father to condescend, to step down and assume mortal flesh as a baby. What power can be found on earth that would respond to someone great and mighty here who gave it up to become innocent and powerless just as baby's are. He went from power to meekness, vulnerability and helplessness. In this example, He marked the way for us to follow and He marked the way that the Melchizedek priesthood was to be handled. It is, as so many scriptures can attest, by love. In contrast to divine command theory, there is divine motivation theory, and at the center of this theory, the motivation is love. In Doctrine and Covenants 121:41 we read, *"No power or influence can or ought to be maintained by virtue of the priesthood,* **only by persuasion, by longsuffering and meekness, and by love unfeigned.***"* These are the hallmarks of the Melchizedek priesthood and the conditions upon which the keys of the priesthood are exercised.

It is clear from the verses cited above in the Old Testament, the New Testament and the Book of Mormon that the Law of Moses was never intended to be permanent; it was fulfilled in the coming of our Savior in mortality at the meridian of time, by His resurrection. The new covenant, found in the New Testament replaced it. Thus, the higher priesthood was restored with the birth of the Savior. This Melchizedek priesthood replaced the Law of Moses. But it did not replace the Aaronic priesthood, which still provided a preparatory priesthood so that men could accept this higher priesthood and higher law while yet preparing themselves and their hearts through the Aaronic preparatory priesthood and its ordinances. Things that pertain to this lesser priesthood are for example the authority to baptize and of particular interest, the gift of the ministering of angels. Is it not clear that these things are given to prepare us, even through divine command theory, to receive the higher law through divine motivation theory, love? Therefore, there was to be another, a higher priesthood required, and according to Paul, as shown above, this priesthood was after the order of Melchizedek. Moreover, we know from the Prophet Joseph Smith that all the prophets that ministered to the House of Israel (including the Jews) held this higher or Melchizedek priesthood:

> ...All Priesthood is Melchizedek, but there are different portions or degrees of it. That portion which brought Moses to speak with God face to face [see Numbers 12:6-8]

was taken away; but that which brought the ministry of angels remained. All the prophets had the Melchizedek Priesthood and were ordained by God himself.

The above tells us that all priesthood is Melchizedek and that the Aaronic priesthood is but an appendage to it. In the Melchizedek priesthood, however, is a fullness of priesthood power and authority articulated. This is why the record of Joseph found in the Book of Mormon contains the fullness of the gospel. How then did the priesthood become divided? We see then, that when the children of Israel were disobedient at Sinai when Moses was delayed in his return from the mountain, they committed great sin. In Exodus 32:17 we read, *"And when Joshua heard the noise of the people as they shouted, he said unto Moses, There is a noise of war in the camp."* In verse 19 we read on further, *"And it came to pass, as soon as he came nigh unto the camp, that he saw the calf, and the dancing: and Moses' anger waxed hot, and he cast the tables out of his hands, and brake them beneath the mount."* The Lord recognized that the children of Israel were not ready to receive the higher law and the higher ordinances contained in a fullness of the Melchizedek priesthood and so another priesthood, a lesser part of the full priesthood, a lesser priesthood was to be given to them.

What this signifies is the House of Israel had rejected the Melchizedek priesthood and the ordinances thereof. The breaking of the tablets signifies that the covenant so recently restored was broken by the House of Israel and with it, the Melchizedek priesthood was taken out of their midst. As the Prophet Joseph Smith indicated, the prophets in the Old Testament held the Melchizedek priesthood because God Himself ordained them. This is very important. Fallen Christianity doesn't believe this. They believe that Jesus Christ alone holds the Melchizedek priesthood, but we then must ask them, "What about Melchizedek?" So why is this so important? The reason is this: only those who hold the Melchizedek priesthood can act in the similitude of the Savior, because their actions are motivated by love for God and not by gaining any earthly reward. It was because Moses held this priesthood that he understood divine motivation theory, if you will, and out of his love for the House of Israel, he thought he could offer himself, even vainly, in an effort to atone for the great sin committed at Sinai (see Exodus 30:30-32 cited below).

Salvation and exaltation come through the Melchizedek priesthood, as we will now demonstrate. But for you, as a missionary, you act through this priesthood and so the Lord has told you in several places, Isaiah 52:7, Romans 10:15, Mosiah 15:17, and in the Doctrine and Covenants 128:19, the following, "*Now, what do we hear in the gospel which we have received? A voice of gladness! A voice of mercy from heaven; and a voice of truth out of the earth; glad tidings for the dead; a voice of gladness for the living and the dead; glad tidings of great joy. How beautiful upon the mountains are the feet of those that bring glad tidings of good things, and that say unto Zion: Behold, thy God reigneth...*" This means that only through this Melchizedek priesthood motivated by love of God and love of our fellowman (Matthew 22:37-40) can the higher ordinances be offered to mankind. "*Jesus said unto him, Thou shalt love the Lord thy God with all thy heart, and with all thy soul, and with all thy mind. This is the first and great commandment. And the second is like unto it, Thou shalt love thy neighbor as thyself.* **On these two commandments hang all the law and the prophets.**" And it is in these higher ordinances, motivated by love, that the love of God will be able to reach its full zenith. It is through these ordinances that the fullness of God's love finds full articulation. Thus, because of this priesthood and the ordinances thereof as motivated by love, tidings of great joy are brought to the earth. This includes the authority to bring about the resurrection of all men as well as the blessings contained in the faith we have in our Savior. We will now discover why.

We can see this fact clearly when we go back and examine what happened at Mt. Sinai when the Lord delivered to Moses His law. As he was detained upon Mt. Sinai, the camp of Israel fell into deep sin. What was this great sin? It was that Israel refused the blessings of the Melchizedek priesthood and its ordinances. Moses knew this and was heartsick. His feet had been upon the mountain, on Mt. Sinai, and he had returned to bring Israel these glad and important tidings. What Moses did next is truly an example to us all. He desired to become a "savior" for his people, the very people for whom he had given so much. He cast himself in the likeness, in the similitude of the Savior. This was just as Peter testified (cited earlier in Acts 3:22), when he said, *"For Moses truly said unto the fathers, A prophet shall the Lord your God raise up unto you of your brethren, like unto me; him shall ye hear and in all things whatsoever he shall say unto you."* Peter was talking in the two previous verses about Jesus Christ. So how is Moses at all like the Savior? We read in Exodus 32:30-32 the answer. *"And it came to pass on the morrow, that Moses said unto the people, Ye have sinned a great sin: and now I will go up unto the Lord; peradventure I shall make an atonement for your sin. And Moses returned unto the Lord, and said, Oh, this people have sinned a great sin, and have made them gods of gold. Yet now, if thou wilt forgive their sin—; and if not, blot me, I pray thee, out of thy book which thou hast written."* Moses was willing to "take the punishment" himself for the House of Israel, so great was his love for them! This is the love that moves God; this is the kind of love for people we must develop if we are to have the temerity, the "cheek" if you will, to ask our investigators to change their lives. We can never ask them to accept the gospel if we are motivated by anything else; we too must be willing to sacrifice ourselves for their well being, not just to acquire a baptismal statistic. Remember, **motive is everything** and the purest motive is this kind of love. Is it not indeed, the pure love of Christ? Is this kind of love not the highest and most wholesome reason to ask someone to embrace our faith? It was in this way that Moses too wanted to take their sins upon him, but of course he couldn't.

    The point is this, he was willing so to do and therefore the Lord heard his plea and did not reject the children of Israel. Instead, they were chastened with plagues, but they were not rejected. They were to be schooled by the lesser priesthood because they were not capable of receiving His love as offered through the higher ordinances of the Melchizedek priesthood. As Paul told the Galatians

(Galatians 3:24) that the Law of Moses was to be a schoolmaster to prepare them to receive His pure love, the very love they had rejected at Sinai, *"Wherefore the law was our schoolmaster to bring us unto Christ, that we might be justified **by faith.**"* It is clear then, that through this pure love of Christ, Moses had power in the priesthood to deliver Israel, even a complaining and often faithless Israel to the Promised Land. It was this lack of faith that precluded the House of Israel from receiving the great gift of love and healing, offered only through the ordinances of the Melchizedek priesthood. This is why the Melchizedek priesthood and the ordinances thereof are so important. But if this priesthood is not empowered by such love and undergirded by great faith, as we read in Doctrine and Covenants 84:20-23, we cannot have power to convert or power to exalt anyone. We read, *"Therefore, in the ordinances thereof, the power of godliness is manifest. And without the ordinances thereof, and the authority of the priesthood, the power of godliness is not manifest unto men in the flesh; For without this no man can see the face of God, even the Father, and live. Now this Moses plainly taught to the children of Israel in the wilderness, and sought diligently to sanctify his people that they might behold the face of God."* Why is this important? The Savior could indeed take their sins upon Him and He in fact did so; but because Moses wanted so to do, he is in the similitude of the Son (meaning in the likeness of the Savior). That is the way we bring the Savior's attention to our work, through this pure love of Christ, as demonstrated by Moses. This gift of charity is magnified in the ordinances of the Melchizedek priesthood as they call us to a state of being in the similitude of the Savior.

Moses had received this love as a gift because he brought forth a sacrifice of a broken heart and a contrite spirit; the very sacrifice we have talked about over and over again in my letters to you. As a missionary, this is an ideal time to learn to be meek. It is not always easy, but so much depends on this trait. Without it, we cannot learn the great mysteries of godliness; without it, power in the priesthood is diminished, and without it, we run a great risk of misunderstanding the mind of the Lord. Meekness is the opposite of pride, the greatest of sins and as we will learn in Volume II, pride creates contention and contention creates apostasy. It is not by coincidence then, that Moses was meek. In Numbers 12:3, we learn, *"Now the man Moses was very meek, above all the men which were upon the face of the earth."* We have already learned that the sacrifice of a broken heart and a contrite spirit is required so that we can receive the gift of faith; it is also required to receive the gift of charity. The gifts that come to us by virtue of the Melchizedek priesthood are ones that cannot be worked on. In other words, gifts such as faith, love and charity cannot be defined by process. No one understands love, faith, or charity in terms of developing these attributes. They are "state of being" attributes that come to us as gifts because of the broken heart and the contrite spirit. It was Elder Dallin H. Oaks, who explained why this is so. He said in part, "The reason charity is greater than even the most significant acts of goodness is that charity is not an act, but a condition or state of being. Charity is something one becomes." ("The Challenge to Become," *Ensign* November 2000, page 34.) This means we do not "work on charity." We become charitable through the grace and goodness of Christ; it is an attribute we acquire as a gift because, like the gift of faith, we bring forth the sacrifice of a broken heart. It is through this sacrifice that we become meek.

Moses is not the only example of love and charity to which we can refer. We read in Alma 13:16-18 about the ordinances and the pure love of Christ, *"Now these ordinances were given after this manner, that thereby the people might look forward on the Son of God, it being a type of his order, or it being his order, and this that they might look forward to him for a remission of their sins, that they might enter into the rest of the Lord. Now this Melchizedek was a king over the land of Salem; and his people had waxed strong in iniquity and abomination; yea, they had all gone astray; they were full of all manner of wickedness; But Melchizedek having exercised mighty faith, and received the office of the high priesthood according to the holy order of God, did preach repentance unto his people. And behold, they did repent; and Melchizedek did establish peace in the land in his days; therefore he was called the prince of peace..."* We note here that Melchizedek "exercised mighty faith."

How could he do this without being meek and how could he be meek without the sacrifice of a broken heart and a contrite spirit? It would not be possible, as we have so thoroughly demonstrated in the prior 9 letters; it always comes back to the broken heart and the contrite spirit.

Faith and meekness give us power in the priesthood to accomplish all things the Lord wants us to do. Think of Nephi's faith and his meekness when we read in 3 Nephi 7:18, *"And it came to pass that they were angry with him, even because he had greater power than they, for it were not possible that they could disbelieve his words, for so great was his faith on the Lord Jesus Christ that angels did minister unto him daily."* Knowing this, you will never read the book of 3 Nephi the same way ever again. Once you recognize the power that is in faith and meekness, you will never approach people you wish to teach and bring to a knowledge of Christ the same way again either! As you learn to use the tools taught to you by your mission leaders, if they are not handled with a broken heart and a contrite spirit, they could produce pride in yourself. If this happens, your testimony of the truth will ring hollow and it will not be sufficient to change lives. This is what Paul meant when he said in 1 Corinthians 13:1, *"Though I speak with the tongues of men and angels, and have not charity, I am become as sounding brass, or a tinkling cymbal."*

Without meekness, there will be no charity and instead of a message that will move men and women to adopt the similitude of Christ and embrace Him. Instead, we become filled with hollowness, even that of harshness, of sounding brass! Such an approach will not move men and women to embrace the Master, our only true leader and our Redeemer. As we live in an ever-increasingly secular world, without such a sacrifice, even the sacrifice of Moses and Melchizedek, Nephi, and I might add Enoch and Abraham to these great men who also were meek and had a broken heart and a contrite spirit, great conversions were not possible. It was because of this sacrifice that the people heard their words. Ammon and his brethren also followed these examples. Because they too understood such a sacrifice of a broken heart and a contrite spirit brings with it the gift of charity, they too desired only to be servants to King

Lamoni and his father. Even if being servants required them to remain with the Lamanites all the days of their lives to accomplish the Lord's purposes (Alma 17:23).

This then brings us to the unparalleled parable of the prodigal son. We read it in Luke 15, beginning in verses 11-13, *"And he said, A certain man had two sons: And the younger of them said to his father, Father, give me the portion of goods that falleth to me. And he divided unto them his living. And not many days after the younger son gathered all together, and took his journey into a far country, and there wasted his substance with riotous living."* This seems to be an all to familiar story. The younger son arrogantly took his inheritance and wasted it; this is symbolic of falling away and becoming disillusioned with the gifts the father had bestowed upon him. This is not unlike many today who find the gospel has become irrelevant to them. As is the case with many of such people, they spend their lives in riotous worldly living. They find it exciting and exhilarating. But in every instance whether in this life or the next, they find such a lifestyle, in the long run, to be bankrupt. So it was with the younger son.

Let's pick up the narrative in verses 17-24, *"And when he came to himself, he said, How many hired servants of my father's have bread enough and to spare, and I perish with hunger! I will arise and go to my father, and will say unto him, Father, I have sinned against heaven, and before thee, And am no more worthy to be called thy son: make me as one of thy hired servants. And he arose, and came to his father.* **But when he was yet a great way off,** *his father saw him, and had compassion, and ran, and fell on his neck, and kissed him. And the son said unto him, Father, I have sinned against heaven, and in thy sight, and am no more worthy to be called thy son. But the father said to his servants, Bring forth the best robe, and put it on him; and put a ring on his hand, and shoes on his feet: And bring hither the fatted calf, and kill it; and let us eat, and be merry: For this my son was dead, and is alive again; he was lost, and is found..."*

What do we learn from these verses? We learn that the son discovered his error and desired to repent. Was this not also the case with Alma as he listened to Abinadi? The younger son felt that all was lost and that he had forever forfeited his birthright as well as his inheritance. He came with a broken heart and a contrite spirit to his father, who as we learned from the next verses, was also possessed of these traits. The father saw him a long way off, perhaps as he cried out in meekness and humility that he was willing to accept a lesser portion, but just wanted to be near his father for he knew that there, he would find some form of salvation. This is analogous to the pleadings of King David who had sinned even in a greater way. David received the promise that the Lord would not leave his soul in hell (see Psalms 86:13), but to the prodigal, he could return.

It is important to realize the father came to him first and in the similitude of the Savior, put a robe on his shoulders and shoes on his feet. Even more importantly, the father put a ring on his younger son's hand signifying that he was not a servant but again an heir. This was accomplished through the pure love of Christ and the faith the father had in his Lord. The father knew of his son's sincere repentance and forgave him and restored him as an heir. We ask, an heir of what? The younger son was restored to his former place and would be able, because of the ring the father put on his hand, to recover his own inheritance. This is very significant because in verses 25-32, the elder son was angry. *"Now his elder son was in the field: and as he came and drew nigh to the house, he heard musick and dancing. And he called one of the servants, and asked what these things meant. And he said unto him, Thy brother is come; and thy father hath killed the fatted calf, because he hath received him safe and sound. And he was angry, and would not go in: therefore came his father out, and entreated him. And he answering said to his father, Lo, these many years do I serve thee, neither transgressed I at any time thy commandment: and yet thou never gavest me a kid, that I might make merry with my friends: But as soon as this thy son was come, which hath devoured thy living with harlots, thou hast killed for him the fatted calf. And he said unto him, Son, thou art ever with me, and all that I have is thine. It was meet that we should make merry, and be glad: for this thy brother was dead, and is alive again; and was lost, and is found."*

The father had no intention of dividing the inheritance again.

All that he then possessed belonged to the elder son, as his portion was not squandered in riotous worldly living. However, the younger son would not need to receive any of what the elder son was going to inherit. Through sincere repentance on his part, and because the father through his own broken heart and contrite spirit as illustrated by the father's desire to rescue his son, brought the son to the point where hope was restored. It was through the compassion of the father and because of the father's pure love for the younger son that change in the prodigal came about. It was because of compassion and through the pure love of Christ found in the father that he was true and faithful to the trust our Savior placed in him. He was willing just as our Savior did, to step down, to condescend if you will, to help the younger son recover his own inheritance. It would be through the "ring of the father," meaning through his gift, that the younger son could once again find himself cleansed and empowered to retrieve all that was once his. The elder son was also taught a great lesson; don't be prideful and arrogant. He said he never transgressed the father's commandments. Is that true? Who on earth has ever not sinned? The answer to this question is obvious and because the elder son has made this arrogant remark, it invoked a quiet but kind rebuke from his father. We should indeed make merry when even one repents and returns to the fold (see the parable of the lost sheep in Luke 15:4-7, an important parable preceding that of the prodigal son).

These parables found in the Gospel of Luke, the parable of the lost sheep and the parable of the prodigal son have far-reaching implications into the world of spirits. We do not know all things concerning this world, but these parables hold out that the spirit world should be filled with hope for all sinners. However, if we choose to live unworthily and use the priesthood unworthily, unlike the prodigal son who came to himself, then at the judgment day, it may be worse for us because the gift of the Atonement will have been rejected. I think that the Lord will be true and faithful to Himself and that He will understand all of the mitigating circumstances as to why this is so. With respect to the priesthood and its unworthy exercise, however, the judgment of such behavior is left to Him, but we must realize, as did King David, that there comes a time when sought-after blessings cannot be recovered. Hopefully these times are rare, but there is a point of no return; so let us help those who exercise the priesthood unworthily to come to themselves, as did the prodigal son.

The true love of Christ, the love of a parent for a child, the meekness and contrite spirit of the valiant are powerful tools magnified by the priesthood as shown by the father in the parable of the prodigal son. Nevertheless, the possibility of forfeiture of blessings exists. Since we know the Lord's desire is to save us all, I will trust that His love is certainly capable of providing to us rescue, but such rescue comes with a condition. Will we want it then as the prodigal son did? To help us along the road, let us hope we too have a father, a mentor, a Melchizedek priesthood holder who will be willing to step into the role of acting in the similitude of the Savior and find it deep within his soul to be a "savior on Mt. Zion"; one whose feet are blessed to go and bring us peace that comes only in Him.

To conclude, there are a number of important lessons found within this letter. One of these is that the Melchizedek priesthood is part of the birthright of the tribe of Joseph, but since all priesthood is Melchizedek, it belongs to the entire family of Abraham, Isaac and Jacob. Through it and through the ordinances of this priesthood, the blessings of Abraham, secured by a covenant between God and Abraham, are made available to all the families of the world. Another important lesson is that the keys of this priesthood, along with the authority given by the laying on of hands (ordaining) are absolutely necessary to confer, direct, and secure the blessings of God for the family of God. As the children of Adam accepted His gospel, they become, through baptism, members of the family of Abraham and thereby an heir to eternal life if they keep the covenants of this priesthood. The keys of the Melchizedek priesthood, held anciently by Adam, Enoch, and then after the flood by Noah, Elijah and others like John the Baptist. These keys were delivered in the meridian of time to Peter, James, and John who administered the church of Christ in former days.

Now in these latter days, and in a like manner, by these same beings, the Melchizedek priesthood was restored to the earth in our day. Peter, James, and John returned to give Joseph Smith and Oliver Cowdery those very same keys, as did Moses, Elijah and certainly John the Baptist.

And finally, when we obtain this priesthood, it is only through bringing forth a broken heart and a contrite spirit that its power can be made manifest in us. Even though our priesthood is valid, it truly becomes legitimate only based on the principles of love, the absolute divine motivator. It is by the power manifested through this priesthood that the world will be changed even if only one life at a time. Such change wrought in the hearts of men can only be accomplished if we too are broken hearted; such a condition in us is a gift. This is a gift we cannot "earn" or "work on" to acquire. It is given freely to those who have taken the yoke of the Savior upon themselves. This yoke is to accept Him as the ultimate gift in whom all problems of mortality are resolved; all pain, all anger, all disease, all disadvantages of being taken advantage of by others, all of these are swallowed up in Him. We accept Him as recompense for all these wrongs. Such power to change lives and bring back the wayward is indeed the work of salvation; it is through this power that true conversion comes and it is through this power that the Lord sanctified His sacrifice to the Father. This sacrifice allowed Him to be both our advocate and our judge. He is meek and lowly of heart and because He loves us and bought us with His blood (Acts 20:28), it is then to Him that we owe our allegiance, yea even our all.

With an abiding faith in the Lord and in His priesthood, I am your brother,

LETTER ELEVEN

THE RIGHT MUST SERVE THE GOOD

*In our effort to be good ambassadors for God, we often overlook
a pivotal understanding of this important self-evident truth.
The right must serve the good of the individual as well
as the good of society, or it is not right.*

Dear Missionary,

I really enjoyed hearing from you. It was good to know that things are much better at the Missionary Training Center and that you seem to be moving into mission life well. I can see that you are growing and that the work of being a missionary seems to agree with you as you are getting "the hang" of missionary work. It was really wonderful when you described the events of the young missionary convert who, when he was investigating the church, told you how the Spirit worked on him and brought him to a knowledge of the truth. You said that you have never seen anyone feel the Spirit like that before and that it was great. I have seen great growth in you and I have seen the Spirit expand you and stretch you. In a way, we could use our experience at the Missionary Training Center to prepare us for an athletic contest. There is a certain fact drawn from athletics that applies here. We know that we seem to play better when we play teams that are better than we are. It seems that when we only play against those teams that are inferior to our team or against those that are equal to our team, we don't grow. It is only when we play against teams that are reported to be better than we are, that we grow and get better. I see this in you.

When you were away at school, I worried that some of the spiritual growth others were having was not coming to you. I noticed that you were not being stretched out, weren't being spiritually challenged to learn and grow as much as if you had been at home. I now see that great talent of yours, never to give up, coming through loud and clear. You have pushed hard and have given it your all, up to now, and you are beginning to see the growth that I always knew was in you. You mentioned you have now been a witness to the workings of the Spirit in someone else. I want you to know that I have seen the same workings of the Spirit generally, but specifically in you these past couple of months. You will see many such miracles in your mission and I know the Lord will continue to teach you many things as you seek to magnify those gifts He has given to you.

I have to tell you about one of your other friends. As you know, he was in the Missionary Training Center about 20 days and the MTC is a big place so you don't know this yet, but he was sent home. You may have heard rumors about it from other people, but I wanted to talk to you a little about this. It seems that this missionary didn't tell the stake president everything about their life and so, after about 20 days in the MTC, this missionary was released and sent home. He has come to me, with the blessing of his stake president, and I have met with him quite a few times. He is embarrassed, because he did not really comprehend the reasons for going on a mission, but more importantly, he didn't understand how the Atonement works. This is why confession is necessary, and what he must do to have the Spirit of forgiveness with him so that he can be pure. You and I have already discussed the subjects of justification and sanctification and I will now discuss these with him. His stake president feels he will be able to return to the mission field, and so I have told him to "hang in" there and make it his goal to return to the mission field as soon as he is able and worthy to do so. I know his stake president well and he will work with this young man to achieve what is best for him and for the church. This incident serves as the perfect analogy for a truth that should be self-evident, but is often hidden from us: the *right* must serve the *good*. This is one principle the stake president will use to help this young man repent, turn around, and if possible, return to the mission field. If this cannot happen, even then, the right must serve the good for healing to take place.

To that end and as I read your letter, I would like to begin with a few lines from Viktor Frankl. Here Frankl, who was a concentration camp survivor, left us a timeless message. What you are facing now as your mission progresses is precisely the reason I wanted you to read this book before you left on your mission. You will remember he tells us, after they first arrived at the camps and had all been told to strip naked:

> Next we were herded into another room to be shaved: not only our heads were shorn, but not a hair was left on our entire bodies. Then on to the showers, where we lined up again. We hardly recognized each other, but with great relief some people noted that real water dripped from the sprays.
>
> While we were waiting for the shower, our nakedness was brought home to us: we really had nothing now except our bare bodies - even minus hair; all we possessed, literally, was our naked existence. What else remained for us as a material link with our former lives? (*Man's Search for Meaning*, page 28.)

They had been reduced to nothing. Identity was just a number; and there was no dignity or humanity left among them. But Frankl goes on to tell us something that is extremely meaningful. In extremis, we learn that the good must serve the right. Frankl then teaches us:

> But I did not only talk of the future and the veil which was drawn over it. I also mentioned the past; all its joys, and how its light shone even in the present darkness. Again I quoted a poet - to avoid sounding like a preacher myself - who had written, "Was Du erlebst, kann keine Macht der Welt Dir rauben." (What you have experienced, no power on earth can take from you.) Not only our experiences, but
>
> all we have done, whatever great thoughts we may have had, and all we have suffered, all this is not lost, though it

is past; we have brought it into being. Having been is also a kind of being, and perhaps the surest kind.

Then I spoke of the many opportunities of giving life a meaning. I told my comrades (who lay motionless, although occasionally a sigh could be heard) that human life, under any circumstances, never ceases to have a privation, meaning that this infinite meaning of life includes suffering and dying, and death. I asked the poor creatures who listened to me attentively in the darkness of the hut to **face themselves** up to the seriousness of our position. They must not lose hope but should keep their courage in the certainty that the hopelessness of our struggle did not detract from its dignity and its meaning. I said that someone looks down on each of us in difficult hours – a friend, a wife, somebody alive or dead, or a God - and he would not expect us to disappoint him. He would hope to find us suffering proudly - not miserably - knowing how to die.

And finally I spoke of sacrifice, which had meaning in every case. It was in the nature of this sacrifice that it should appear to be pointless in the normal world, the world of material success. But in reality our sacrifice did have a meaning. Those of us who had any religious **faith**, I said frankly, could understand without difficulty...The purpose of my words was to find a full meaning in our life, then and there, in that hut and in that practically hopeless situation. I saw that my efforts had been successful. (*Man's Search for Meaning*, page 90.)

Then, finally Frankl quotes a passage from Nietzsche, a great German philosopher: "**He who knows a 'why' to live for can bear with almost any how**" (*Man's Search for Meaning,* page 85). Frankl's experiences are applicable, even if they were extreme, to life in the Missionary Training Center and eventually into the mission field itself. The meaning of this experience will not be lost on you if you live your life with virtue and seek the justifying companionship of the Holy Ghost.

There is a larger question here, which you are confronting. There is a conflict, perhaps inherent in this world in which we live, which sometimes pits two virtues against each other. These virtues are the "right" and the "good." Some favor the "right" over the "good" while others place the "good" over the "right." It is a tough call. How do we define the right and how do we define the good? We look to the Thirteenth Article of Faith for a suitable definition of the good. We read:

> We believe in being honest, true, chaste, benevolent, virtuous, and in doing good to all men; indeed, we may say that we follow the admonition of Paul—We believe all things, we hope all things, we have endured many things, and hope to be able to endure all things. If there is anything virtuous, lovely, or of good report or praiseworthy, we seek after these things.

The good deals with outcomes that are honest, virtuous, and filled with hope and equity. The greatest good is to bring to pass the immortality and eternal life of man (Moses 1:39). It is to that end that the good is dedicated. To that end, we read in 1 Nephi of the death of Laban. Nephi recoiled at taking his life, but was constrained by the Lord to do it, even in light of the commandment not to kill. As Nephi searched for answers, the Lord told him in verse 4:13, *"Behold, the Lord slayeth the wicked to bring forth his righteous purposes. It is better that one man should perish than that a nation should dwindle and perish in unbelief."* What do we learn from this verse? It becomes very clear that even though it is wrong to kill, when the good is in conflict with the right the good always prevails. We see this when the Lord uses the words, "it is better that." This tells us that as far as He is concerned, the right should serve the good. Why? It is because the equities of salvation would be thwarted; the purposes of God, the virtuous, the lovely and those things of good report would be repudiated.

Now let us look at a definition of the right. Here we find some common ground with the good. We see that the purpose of the right is to produce justice. Justice can also be defined as equity. We might say that a complementary definition of the right is also to create equity by our good behavior. If this is so, then when the right and the good come into conflict, the equity of the situation prescribes that the good should be taken into higher consideration; in other words, the right must serve the good, just as the example of Nephi and Laban show. Another example of this is found in Genesis 12:11-13, *"And it came to pass, when he was* come near to enter into Egypt, that he said unto Sarai his wife, Behold now, I know that thou art a fair woman to look upon: Therefore it shall come to pass, when the Egyptians shall see thee, that they shall say, This is his wife: and they will kill me, but they will save thee alive. Say, I pray thee, thou art my sister: that it may be well with me for thy sake; and my soul shall live because of thee." Here Abraham was told to lie to Pharaoh's soldiers to preserve the greater good that God sought to bring to pass through Abraham, namely the salvation of mankind! Again, the good must serve the right so that the equities of God are preserved. In that light of the right, let us read Isaiah 11:4, *"But with righteousness shall he judge the poor, and reprove with equity for the meek of the earth: and he shall smite the earth with the rod of his mouth, and with the breath of his lips shall he slay the wicked."*

We return now to the conundrum faced by our friend who is now at home, but hoping to recover himself. Let us look more deeply at this principle by first seeking out a further example. In John 8:3-12, *"And the scribes and Pharisees brought unto him a woman taken in adultery; and when they had set her in the midst, They say unto him, Master, this woman was taken in adultery, in the very act. Now Moses in the law commanded us, that such should be stoned: but what sayest thou? This they said, tempting him, that they might have to accuse him. But Jesus stooped down, and with his finger wrote on the ground, as though he heard them not. So when they continued asking him, he lifted up himself, and said unto them, He that is without sin among you, let him first cast a stone at her. And again he stooped down, and wrote on the ground. And they which heard it, being convicted by their own conscience, went out one by one, beginning at the eldest, even unto the last: and Jesus was left alone, and the woman standing in the midst. When Jesus had lifted up himself, and saw none but the woman, he said unto her, Woman, where are those thine accusers? hath no man condemned thee? She said, No man, Lord. And Jesus said unto her, Neither do I condemn thee: go, and sin no more."*

It is interesting to note that she was not shamed, nor ridiculed, nor made to feel guilty, as would be the case with those who worship the law instead of the Lord. The Savior told her that He did not condemn her, but that she should "go thy way and sin no more." He did not even call her "wicked" or "rebellious" because she did not need chastening. She was neither wicked nor rebellious and simply needed to feel the love of the Lord and be moved to repent. Through that love, she would find confidence in Him and develop a broken heart and a contrite spirit. Offering those sacrifices to the Lord, faith would have been born. The first fruits of faith are repentance (the second principle of the gospel). With sincere repentance, the Savior absolutely would **forgive** her and she would be healed. In fact, in the Joseph Smith translation, verse 11 ends with these words, *"And the woman glorified God from that hour, and believed on his name."*

There is another great illustration of this point given in Luke 7:36-48. I will quote these verses, though they are long, because they are so very instructive of this principle. We read, *"And one of the Pharisees desired him that he would eat with him. And he went into the Pharisee's house, and sat down to meat. And, behold, a woman in the city, which was a sinner, when she knew that Jesus sat at meat in the Pharisee's house, brought an alabaster box of ointment, And stood at his feet behind him weeping, and began to wash his feet with tears, and did wipe them with the hairs of her head, and kissed his feet, and anointed them with the ointment. Now when the Pharisee which had bidden him saw it, he spake within himself, saying, This man, if he were a prophet, would have known who and what manner of woman this is that toucheth him: for she is a sinner. And Jesus answering said unto him, Simon, I have somewhat to say unto thee. And he saith, Master, say on."* The stage is now set; just as with the woman taken in adultery, this woman sought redemption. She recognized in Jesus the very person who could grant her relief from her sinful burdens and she demonstrates great faith in waiting upon Him and serving His needs. Notice, she didn't ask him for anything but like Mary, in the case of Lazarus (as we have already discussed), waited upon the Lord, recognizing in Him the very relief she sought.

Let us read on and see how our Lord dealt with this sinful

woman, because she is indeed emblematic of all of us. As usual, the Savior taught a parable to Simon the Pharisee to see if he could understand that the good must serve the right, *"There was a certain creditor which had two debtors: the one owed five hundred pence, and the other fifty. And when they had nothing to pay, he frankly forgave them both. Tell me therefore, which of them will love him most? Simon answered and said, I suppose that he, to whom he forgave most. And he said unto him, Thou hast rightly judged. And he turned to the woman, and said unto Simon, Seest thou this woman? I entered into thine house, thou gavest me no water for my feet: but she hath washed my feet with tears, and wiped them with the hairs of her head. Thou gavest me no kiss: but this woman since the time I came in hath not ceased to kiss my feet. My head with oil thou didst not anoint: but this woman hath anointed my feet with ointment.* **Wherefore I say unto thee, Her sins, which are many, are forgiven; for she loved much: but to whom little is forgiven, the same loveth little***. And he said unto her, Thy sins are forgiven."*

We learn from this experience that the Lord does not have any desire to condemn any of us. He desires that we repent and shows that those who have greater sin have the greater need. When we think about it, we are reminded of the words of Paul who said (Romans 3:10-12), *"And it is written, There is none righteous, no, not one: There is none that understandeth, there is none that seeketh after God...There is none that doeth good, no, not one."* He further links forgiveness with love. What kind of love? Love for God and for mankind, as we have so often discussed previously. Remember, the words of the Savior (Matthew 22:40) that on these two, *"hang all the law and the prophets."*

What is happening here again is the Lord is pointing out that the right must serve the good and the right must be governed by love. Thus the Lord is telling us: a thing might be right and not serve the good and therefore it becomes wrong. For example, obedience without faith and love may be, strictly construed, to be right; however, it rarely serves the good because when obedience is rendered just to be right, it is often done in arrogance and pride. These traits are **never** good. The Lord forgave this woman because she had a broken heart and a contrite spirit as demonstrated by her own behavior. She relied totally on Him and realized that her works could not "earn" or "buy" salvation let alone exaltation. It was because of her faith and her love of God that the Lord was moved, not because of any hyper-obedience or good works. She still needed to repent and probably needed to be baptized in order to realize the promise of the Lord. He was certain she would indeed do these things, and based upon His knowledge of her, and because He was moved by her faith in Him, He forgave her, even though she probably owed "five hundred pence," while the unforgiving Simon may have only owed "fifty!" Simon was filled with pride, and that pride would eventually cost him dearly. What a lesson! What majesty there is in faith and in love and what power!

I have gone on too long, my dear friend, but I want you to know that the right must serve the good or it is not right; this is not understood by many. The fact that it is so was the key relationship that caused Viktor Frankl to come to understand the "will to meaning." All experience can serve the good even if at the beginning it is wrong or not good. The Lord as recorded in the Doctrine and Covenants 122:7 told Joseph Smith the following, *"And if thou shouldst be cast into the pit…if the very jaws of hell shall gape open the mouth wide after thee, know thou, my son, that all these things shall give thee experience, and shall be for thy **good**."* It is always wisdom to weigh the right with the good as Solomon truly learned. In Proverbs 2:6-9 we read, *"For the LORD giveth wisdom: out of his mouth cometh knowledge and understanding. He layeth up sound wisdom for the righteous: he is a buckler to them that walketh uprightly. He keepeth the paths of judgment, and preserveth the way of his saints. Then shalt thou understand **righteousness, and judgment, and equity**; yea, every good path."* And if we observe this proverb, Solomon concludes with this (Proverbs 3:27), **"Withhold not good from them to whom it is due, when it is in the power of thine hand to do it."**

My dear friend, I would never change you. You are one who sees; you are a person with faith, born of a broken heart and a contrite spirit. You are on this mission for the right reasons: love of God and love of your fellow man. You know the good and therefore make the right serve the good. Others have not yet learned this. Be patient and the Lord will deliver to you a great victory. You are in the prayers of loved ones every day, I know the Lord is very mindful of you and will use you to further His cause in unusual ways. Be cheerful, and remember the eleventh commandment, "do not take thyself too darn seriously." This is the time to serve the Lord and to *"becometh as a child, submissive, meek, humble, patient, full of love, willing to submit to all things which the Lord seeth fit to inflict...*(upon you) *even as a child doth submit to his father."* (Mosiah 3:19). I hope by now your preparations are in full force and that things are well on the way to launch you successfully into your field of labor. Preparation will continue in the field itself, but for now, you are ready.

When you get home, you will find yourself with a collection of experiences that will contain both good and bad ones. In fact, as we go through life we collect memories, and in the end, memories are all that remain. So, if along the way we build these memories, many of them coming with the realization that the Holy Ghost has repeatedly touched our spirits, these memories will then serve us well. They will have been the catalyst by which we will remember how to learn by the Spirit and how to become justified before the Lord. With the justification of our efforts, the memories will be sweet indeed. Those that are good will be placed in contrast to the bad. As you review these experiences, I want you to go to the Lord in prayer and seek His approbation. Seek the justifying power of the Holy Ghost to seal your efforts. A great key to be able to receive this blessing is found in the principle, of the good versus the right. If you have learned this principle while in the mission field, you will be a better-prepared servant to continue to serve in the kingdom of God. Through the principle of the good serving the right, you will come to know the Master because you will have served Him as He serves us. Mosiah 5:13 tells us, *"For how knoweth a man the master whom he has not served, and who is a stranger unto him, and is far from the thoughts and intents of his heart?"*

Truly when we allow the right to serve the good, we know the Master, for this is what He did. This principle will further inspire you to know of the truthfulness of the doctrine you will teach as John tells us in John 7:17, *"If any man will do his will, he shall know of the doctrine, whether it be of God, or whether I speak of myself."* We will make sense out of all of it, but for now serve with all *"your heart, might, mind and strength."*

I would like to leave you with one last scripture before you depart for the mission field. It certainly pertains to this important concept of the right serving the good. Early in this dispensation, as missionaries went out into the field, the Lord challenged them as follows in Doctrine and Covenants 35:14, *"And their arm shall be my arm, and I will be their shield and their buckler; and I will gird up their loins, and they shall **fight manfully for me;** and their enemies shall be under their feet; and I will let fall the sword in their behalf, and by the fire of mine indignation will I preserve them."*

I know that if you give this mission all you have to give and work as a humble servant, seeking the grace of God in your life to enable you to do His work, the good that is reflected in your life will be filled with the right. As you now enter the mission field properly, you will have new questions. These will come from investigators, members, and of course from other missionaries. Refer back to the letters found in this Volume I to further solidify your foundation. As your preparation continues and your MTC experience comes to a close, look to the answers found in Letters to Missionaries: Volume II. These letters are pertinent to the field and will help you with missionary work in your relevant area. Put the knowledge learned from Volume II in a different context, as the thrust of these new letters will be different, albeit the fundamentals of a broken heart and a contrite spirit will remain the same. The right must always serve the good especially as you begin your journey in the mission field as a servant of God. May the Lord preserve you and your companions with His almighty hand. His Spirit will be upon you and you will find peace and rest in His wonderful service.

With deep personal regards,

BIBLIOGRAPHY

Ashton, Marvin J. *The Measure of our Heart.* Salt Lake City: Deseret Book, 1991.

Ballard, M. Russell. "Missionary Work." Address given at the University of Utah Institute of Religion, October 15, 2006.

Conference Reports of the Church of Jesus Christ of Latter-day Saints. Salt Lake City: The Church of Jesus Christ of Latter-day Saints, October 2007, October 1949, April 1989, October 1984, April 2009, April 1960.

Cannon, George Q. *Gospel Truth: Discourses of George Q. Cannon.* Jerreld L. Lundquist, ed., Salt Lake City: Deseret Book, 1987.

Clark, J. Reuben. *Why the King James Version.* Salt Lake City: Deseret Book, 1979.

Frankl, Viktor. *Man's Search for Meaning.* Boston: Beacon Press, 2006.

Journal of Discourses. 26 vols. Liverpool: F. D. Richards and Sons, 1855-1886.

Kimball, Spencer W. Remarks given at the European Area Conference, Paris, France, August, 1976.

Kipling, Rudyard. *The Oxford Book of English Verse 1250-1900.* Ed. Arthur Quiller-Couch. Oxford: Claredon Press, 1919.

Lee, Harold B. *Stand Ye in Holy Places.* Salt Lake City: Deseret Book, 1971.

Maxwell, Neal A. *Meek and Lowly.* Salt Lake City: Deseret Book, 1987.

McConkie, Bruce R. *Mormon Doctrine.* Salt Lake City: Bookcraft, 1966.

_____*Doctrinal New Testament Commentary.* 3 volumes. Salt Lake City: Bookcraft, 1971.

McConkie, Joseph Fielding. *Straightforward Answers to Tough Gospel Questions.* Salt Lake City: Deseret Book, 1998.

Monson, Thomas S. "Who Honors God, God Honors." *Ensign,* November 1995.

Mother Teresa. *Come Be My Light: The Private Writings of the "Saint of Calcutta."* Ed. Brian Kolodiejchuk, M. C., New York: Double Day, 2007.

Nibley, Hugh W. "Leaders and Managers." *Speeches* Provo, Utah: Commencement Address. Brigham Young University, August 19, 1983.

Oaks, Dallin H. "The Challenge to Become." *Ensign,* November 2000.

Packer, Boyd K. Address given at a CES Fireside, November 9, 1993.

_____ "What Every Missionary Should Know." Address given at Mission President's Seminar, June 26, 2002.

Smith, Joseph. *Lectures on Faith.* Salt Lake City: Deseret Book, 1985.

Smith, Joseph. *Teachings of the Prophet Joseph Smith.* Comp. Joseph Fielding Smith. Salt Lake City: Deseret Book, 1968.

Smith, Joseph Fielding. *Doctrines of Salvation.* 3 volumes. Comp. Bruce R. McConkie. Salt Lake City: Bookcraft, 1954-1956.

Welch, John and Larry Morris, Eds. *Oliver Cowdery – Scribe, Elder, Witness.* Provo, Utah: The Neal A. Maxwell Institute for Religious Scholarship. Brigham Young University, 2006.

Wirthlin, Joseph B. "Patience, A Key to Happiness." *Ensign,* May 1987.